A 'Desert Rat' Story

George Frame

Narrated by John Frame

Published by New Generation Publishing in 2020

First Edition

ISBN
Paperback	978-1-80031-611-9
Hardback	978-1-80031-610-2
Ebook	978-1-80031-609-6

www.newgeneration-publishing.com

 New Generation Publishing

This book is dedicated to George and Lorraine

George Frame

Cairo 1941

A Desert Rat's Story

Acknowledgements

This is **George's** story written from notes in his diary and from him relaying events and experiences of his time in the Second World War.

Russell Smith assisted with copying the pictures from George's photo album and enhancing them sufficiently to be of acceptable standard for the book. This was not an easy task given these photographs are 75 years old and there are no negatives from which to develop new photographs.

My family, Janet, Chris, Catherine, Alex and Rachelle for supporting me in writing this and my other three books, **RETRIBUTION, PARADIGM of SUCCESS** and **THE RHODESIAN CIVIL WAR (1966-1979).**

Glossary of Terms

Afrika Korps – The name given to the German Army in North Africa

Biltong – Dried meat (jerky)

Bioscope – Cinema

Boys in Blue – Airforce

Foxholes – Term given for dug in defensive positions

Slit Trench – A narrow dug out for soldiers and their equipment

The Front – Where the battles took place

Forward

While written by me, his son, this book tells George's story.

It is a story of his experience in the Second World War. A war in which he volunteered to fight and which for George was played out in North Africa. The naivety of a twenty four year old volunteer and the mind numbing drudgery of military training was quickly swept away by the stark reality of human conflict and what horrific things men at war can do to each other. What George saw and what he experienced is something that was indelibly printed in his mind, living with him until be passed away in 2010, aged 94.

He did not speak about the war that much. A few snippets here and there came out at times. His war time diary, where he had jotted down his experiences in that conflict, was kept pretty much to himself. His photo album, where he had his pictures of the war, was not on display. However, in the last few years of his life he did start to relay more insights to what he had experienced. I took the opportunity to write down notes thinking it would be good to have a record somewhere to pass down to the grandchildren.

This book is a compilation of the notes made from the conversations I had with George and those memories written in his diary.

The pictures in this book are from his collection. Most of these pictures were taken by George himself, while those showing German scenes came from a camera he found lying in the desert.

The book also portrays a love story. His chance meeting with Lorraine Cordner weeks before being shipped out to Egypt, where he fell head over heels in love for the first and only time in his 94 years, set a deep desire within him to get back home alive to marry her. He did get back from the war and they were married for 61 years.

George had a terrific life philosophy. "It's a wonderful life," was his catch cry.

For those of us living in a peaceful democracy, with a rule of law that is fair and equitable, we owe this way of life to those who fought against tyranny and evil. George's generation who sacrificed so much so that we can live as we do should never be forgotten.

Evil succeeds when good people do nothing! George chose to do something and this is his story. Thank you George.

Chaos, fused with fear, often occurred when the bullets started flying in a battle. Generally it occurred sporadically, often weeks apart. Then occasionally it was daily. But whenever it happened it was frightening and one did whatever was necessary to stay alive.

(George Frame)

A 'Desert Rat' Story

Chapter One

"A war to the finish …. A war of national survival for Southern Rhodesia and for Britain. The mother country's defeat would leave little hope for the colony in the post-war world…." were the words said by the Prime Minister of Southern Rhodesia, Godfrey Martin Huggins, 1st Viscount Malvern, when on 3rd September 1939 he issued the Southern Rhodesian declaration of war against Nazi Germany before any other British dominions did.

I was twenty three when Nazi Germany invaded Poland and the United Kingdom declared war.

At that time I was working as a labourer at the Liebig abattoir in West Nicolson, Southern Rhodesia. The abattoir was the main employer in this isolated rural village situated half way between Bulawayo, the second city of Southern Rhodesia, and Beit Bridge, the border crossing over the Limpopo River to South Africa.

It was hard work, especially during the hot months, but the work at Liebig was better than what I had previously experienced at the mines in Northern Rhodesia. I had worked on the mines for a short period before I became very ill with pleurisy which forced me to return home to Bulawayo where my mother nursed me back to health over several months.

The working day was typically ten hours, with half an hour for a lunch break, Monday to Friday, plus every second Saturday which was a half day, knocking off at noon. The meals served up in the mess hall were hearty so there were no complaints in that regard. The accommodation that the Company provided was sparse but adequate. We each had a small room with a window and door, narrow bed, a table and a chair. The bathrooms were shared. An African domestic worker would clean the rooms and bathrooms each day. He did an excellent, diligent job, always with a huge smile.

Liebig Advert (Southern Rhodesian Herald)

Because the place was situated in the bush, there was little to do at West Nicolson, so the evenings were mostly spent at the local hotel bar. I probably drank too much beer. To stave off boredom over the weekends, after work finished on Saturday in the hope to attend a dance, I would drive to Messina, a town in South Africa close to the border, or to Bulawayo. I really enjoyed dancing and fortunately had a group of friends who shared that interest. There were several young ladies with whom I was not romantically involved with but who enjoyed these occasions. Aside from that I would take to the bush to hunt game to supply meat rations for the workforce and to make biltong whenever the opportunity arose.

My car was my main possession. It was a red 1936 Morris Roadster. It was my pride and joy that I was fortunate enough to buy with a loan from my father. It was nippy, yet quite stable on the roads, which were mostly dirt and strip tar. Several years earlier, during the Great Depression, the Southern Rhodesian Government had initiated a road making policy to help employ the men who were out of work. Two parallel strips of tarmac were laid which was cheaper than a full road so the limited Government funds could go further. When passing oncoming traffic, one had to pull off to one side and, depending on the state of the verge, getting back onto the strips could be problematic. As many accidents arose from these roads as it did from hitting wild animals.

Strip Roads in Southern Rhodesia

(George Frame Collection)

6

West Nicolson moved at a sedentary pace, so the news of the world, or of Southern Rhodesia for that matter, was scarce. The radio was available of course, but few newspapers found their way to the village. I don't think many people really cared what was happening outside this little community. For my part I took little interest in what was happening in politics in Southern Rhodesia or the world. My mother had spoken about this fellow Hitler and that it seemed there may well be another war brewing between the United Kingdom and Germany. The First World War was vivid in her memory and I could reflect later on how this would have been bothering her. It meant little to me as I was disinterested in what was happening so far away in Europe. At this time my father was away in Northern Rhodesia working on a mine, but I cannot recall him discussing or even mentioning any matters leading up to the outbreak of the war. He was disinterested in politics as far as I could make out.

On the day Southern Rhodesia declared war on Nazi Germany work stopped at the abattoir so we could hear the Prime Minister of Southern Rhodesia make a solemn speech on the radio. The news was regarded positively and with enthusiasm by the younger white lads. Cheers went up. The black workers had no interest, while some older white chaps looked either sad or worried. The news broke the monotony of the work, if only briefly, and I did not pay much heed to it for quite some time. Some of the lads speculated about the war during our pub sessions, but I had little opinion to offer on the matter other than believing the United Kingdom, the mother country, was bound to win once again.

However, after a while as the news trickled through that Germany had the upper hand and with France falling so quickly leaving Britain standing alone, the discussions amongst the chaps turned towards a need to get involved. The Southern Rhodesian Army that was essentially made up of black Africans and the Air Force chaps, who were all white, had already gone to East Africa and while there was no conscription, many of the lads began considering volunteering. Southern Rhodesia had a shortage of skilled manpower to run the economy and its businesses so conscription was not considered in the best interests of the country which needed to continue to operate the mines and farms to supply Britain with raw materials and food.

My parents never mentioned anything about their three sons going to war, so when I raised the subject about volunteering, my mother in particular, was most unenthusiastic indeed. She argued strongly that the country needed its young men to stay and keep the wheels of commerce turning. Then in more desperation, seeing that I was not being dissuaded, she started explaining how so many young men had sacrificed themselves in the First World War, a war to end all wars, and for what? Two decades later the same participants were fighting again.

Harold, my older brother, who was working as an accounts clerk in Bulawayo, showed no interest at all in joining the army. Douglas, my younger brother, showed interest, but he had lost an eye as a young boy so the chances of him being regarded as fit for the army were slim.

I was at a time in my life where I was looking for something, not exactly knowing what that something was. I really did not know what I wanted to do with my life. Labouring in an abattoir, knee deep in the blood and guts of dead cattle for a meagre wage was not really that enthralling. The work on the mines was hard labour, again for basic wages. I had no formal qualifications, having left school without the school leaver's certificate. At least I could read and write and add up columns of pounds, shillings and pence quickly and accurately, but the thought of being stuck in an office as a clerk, like Harold, for eight to nine hours each day did not fit my desire to be in the outdoors.

I started to understand from conversations amongst the chaps that the Nazis were looking for world domination and there was a growing probability that they would actually beat Britain and then we would all be colonies of the Germans. The indiscriminate bombing of London seemed unjust to me because it was attacking and killing women and children rather than just fighting the army. We started to hear about the Japanese and what they were up to in China and elsewhere which also played on my mind to a lesser degree. I preferred it if things stayed as they were and as British. Albeit I was born in Southern Rhodesia and was to learn we would be regarded as colonialists by the British, we were not going to be told what to do by Germans or Japanese.

Chapter Two

I cannot recall the exact moment I decided to join up, but it was a definite decision that I made.

I did not tell my mother or father until I had attended the recruitment office in Bulawayo and signed the papers, because I knew mother would argue with me and try to persuade me against it. When I did tell her, I could see in her eyes the anguish and disappointment. I felt bad for that, but was glad in myself for having made the decision.

Within a week I got the papers from the Southern Rhodesian Regiment to present myself at their barracks in Salisbury, the capital of Southern Rhodesia, plus a 2nd class train ticket to get from Bulawayo to Salisbury. Leaving the Bulawayo train station, saying goodbye to my mother and two brothers, was sad but that emotion was quickly overtaken by the excitement of adventure. I was going to Salisbury which was a far bigger place than Bulawayo and that exited me.

With a sense of adventure and eager anticipation I walked through the gates of King George VI Barracks. This was the main army barracks situated close to the centre of Salisbury. The place was a buzz of activity with dozens of men, presumably other volunteers, milling around. At ten o'clock an army officer came out to the front of the building and yelled out instructions. We were told to go to the parade ground beyond another gate and to line up into two rows. We certainly looked a strange bunch due to us all wearing different clothes, some in suits and others in casual clothes with long trousers, a few in shorts and each with an assortment of baggage.

After a laconic welcome address, we were marched off in rather a clumsy way to a hall for medicals then, for those who passed, to get kitted out and allocated into our barrack blocks. Other than feeling rather uncomfortable when the doctor held my balls and being asked to cough, an experience I sensed he rather enjoyed more than was needed, the examination was pretty basic. I was classified as fit for general duty. After depositing our kit and bags in the barrack we then had to line up for our hair to be cut. Really short back and sides was the standard.

I really liked the slouch hat we were issued. The regiment's flag was black at the top and green at the base with a thin red line dividing the two and a large red circle in the middle. In the centre of the circle was a Rhodesian heraldic lion holding an ivory tusk, a relic from the British South Africa Company's Coat of Arms. The British South Africa Company had been established by Royal Charter. Cecil Rhodes was the creator and a founding director of the Company as well as Governor of the

Cape. He was exceptionally wealthy from his entrepreneurial skills with diamond and gold mining. The Royal Charter granted the Company the right to explore and occupy lands north of the Limpopo and from that, Southern Rhodesia came about. It was unique in that a Company occupied land in Central Africa establishing a parliamentary system of government.

The Rhodesia Regiment Badge and flag

(George Frame Collection)

That first night I made pals with two chaps who had beds on either side of mine in the barrack block. Both Walter and Taffy would play an important part in my next chapter in life.

Woken at five the next day, I soon realised that was to be the routine for many weeks and this was not going to be a cushy ride. The bed was comfortable enough but the springs squeaked every time I moved. Some chaps snored, so between the squeaking, farting and snoring, I did not have a great night's sleep.

The communal showers were interesting to say the least. Some lads were only too proud to show off their manhood, while others were not that enthusiastic. One lad got the nickname that morning of 'Donkey' and it was not because of his large ears.

After making our beds and dressing into our new uniforms, where some discovered they had imperfect fit, we were introduced to our Warrant Officer. What a prize bastard he turned out to be. Shouting and carrying on, making us do ridiculous things that made no sense and generally being unpleasant as often as he could. Of course I later understood that it was all to dehumanise us and to make us blindly follow orders.

The inspection of our uniforms and how we had made our beds that morning was an arduous affair that lasted several hours. There were only thirty of us in that barrack room. By the end of it my back ached from standing at attention for that long. I had made my bed three times which was actually a successful achievement given what some lads went through. I was not called a mommy's boy, knob, waste of space, piece of crap and other very descriptive words of female anatomy, so I counted myself quite fortunate.

The WO told us because of the shambles from the barrack inspection we had missed breakfast and that we would go straight to parade where we received the riot act on how useless we really were. Then the training regime started.

I thought I was reasonably fit, but was proved wrong pretty quickly. However I was much fitter than most and many poor lads found it really tough going. Luckily I could run quite fast and quickly developed more endurance. Those who were slow, were unfit, argued or did not listen, were punished with greater physical exercise. It was sometimes agonising to see them being put through the hoops, but then at least it was them and not me. The smart chaps quickly learned that as long as some other poor bloke was being hammered by the WO, it meant they were not, except when some idiot really fouled up and we all had to do extra exercise. Those blokes got it in the neck not only from the WO but then special treatment from the rest of us afterwards.

I proved to be a good shot at the rifle range because of my experience with guns from my time in the bush. That got me allocated to artillery training after the basic training was done. I missed the connection between a rifle and a 25 pounder artillery gun in that selection thought process. Anyway firing the artillery guns, although all I did was load artillery shells, was better than firing old .303 rifles in the firing range.

I was rather disappointed that I did not get selected for the officers' training. I suspect that was because I could not show any school qualification. Those lads with degrees or school leaving certificates seemed to be who they selected.

My hope to be selected to go into the Air Force and become a pilot was also dashed. I was very disappointed with that. Looking back, it was fortunate because most of those who went into the Air Force did not come back, especially those who went into Bomber Command. Then those who failed to be a pilot, which on reflection could have been me, ended up as bomber crew and those gunners were almost always the first to be shot to pieces.

Training in the armoured cars in Southern Rhodesia

(George Frame collection)

Armoured Cars in Southern Rhodesia. (George Frame collection)

I finished my training as a private in the artillery and had learned some useful lessons. I had realised very early in the piece that I needed to take orders, jump to it and in that way would blend in and not be targeted. Anyone with a nuance, or who argued, or felt aggrieved would get it in the neck. I learned to work efficiently to do many tasks that would help me survive the war like unhitching and hitching the artillery guns to the trucks, loading the shells into the barrel quickly and replacing wheels very fast.

Training in Southern Rhodesia. George is second from right.

(George Frame collection)

Whenever we got leave passes I went, often with Taffy, to find dance parties in Salisbury and failing that, to the numerous bars around the city. I had no difficulty in approaching young ladies to start chatting with them. I was not the shy sort. A few of the lads soon realised the benefit of having me around when on the prowl for ladies. Consequently I became somewhat popular and was asked to join groups of lads when going into town. At least I got free beers out of it.

Poor old Walter was scared stiff of girls. I had never known anyone like him before. Some big girl must have given him a spanking as a small boy for him to be like he was. Girls and Walter were like water and oil. On the other hand Taffy liked girls a lot but was clumsy, especially with his introduction. He particularly liked dancing but to do that he needed a girl to partner him in the first instance which often proved difficult. So the habit began that I would make the introductions to break the ice and Taffy would come up in the rear, with Walter disappearing.

George's pride and joy. (George Frame collection)

It was rather a carefree time outside of the drudgery of the training and the prospect of what a war would be like had not really entered my thinking. I was not an orphan here either. The other lads really had not given the prospect of being in a battle much thought. I was enjoying a different way of life. Strangely I felt a purpose building in me that I had not experienced before.

Southern Rhodesian Regiment at King George VI Barracks in Salisbury before departure for North Africa

George Frame - 4th from the left, second row. (George Frame collection)

When the training ended we got a weeks' leave before we were to be taken by train to Durban, in South Africa, from where we would be sent to the war by ship. We had not been told where that deployment would be and speculation was rife.

I spent my leave in Bulawayo with my mother and brothers. My parting was very sad indeed, with mother crying. My older brother Harold showed little emotion, while my younger brother, Douglas was upset. I travelled back to Salisbury by train to report in at the Barrack only to board a train the next day that took us back to Bulawayo en-route to South Africa. I had never been on a train so often in such a short period of time before.

Saying farewell to family in Bulawayo before leaving for North Africa. George (second from the right) is in uniform behind his father and mother.

(George Frame collection)

The train line passed through Botswana, then called the Bechuanaland Protectorate, before entering South Africa. I had never been through Bechuanaland before and was surprised how dry and desolate the county was.

We had been told that a group of South African Afrikaners, who were supporters of Germany, had been known to sabotage the rail lines. They believed South Africa should align themselves with Hitler. They probably just still didn't like the British after the Boer War. They were called OB's which stood for some Afrikaans word, Ossewabrandwag, that meant Ox-

Wagon Fireguard. As a result, once the train entered South Africa, it travelled slower and stopped at bridges so they could be inspected for explosives. I was flabbergasted that any South Africans could support the Nazis, but then, the Boers had fought a bitter battle against Britain forty years before and memories can linger for a long time down the generations. While the Boers lost that war and they blamed the British for setting up concentration camps, where many hundreds of their women and children died of diseases, they subsequently won the elections and formed the Government of the Union of South Africa which at that time was still part of the British Commonwealth. The chap who led the Afrikaners in the Boer War, Jan Smuts, even became their Prime Minister. I had heard that if Churchill died Smuts would become the Prime Minister of the United Kingdom. I did not understand how that arrangement had occurred or how it would work out given the bitterness between Afrikaners and the British.

When we arrived in Johannesburg we had to change trains. It was an eye-opener for me to see such a large city. Johannesburg had many skyscrapers which I had never seen the like of before. Once at the station there was no time to do anything else other than change trains and the three of us, Taffy, Walter and I, scrambled to get ourselves into a compartment so we could stay together. I got a top bunk in the four bed compartment.

Two steam trains pulled the carriages from Johannesburg en route to Durban. I spent many hours looking at the countryside as it rolled past. Once we got to the Natal / Transvaal border, the railway line descended one thousand five hundred feet over forty miles as it wound its way through an escarpment and some really lovely country. I particularly liked to see the northern Drakensberg Mountains in the distance when the train slowly manoeuvred through countless hills and across deep river valleys. I was hoping to spot some wildlife but I didn't see any, much to my disappointment.

Looking out at the scenery I thought how beautiful it was and remembered a book that I had read which described Natal as a blood stained Eden. Many bitter battles had been fought in this country between the Zulu tribe and other African tribes as they fought to subjugate them, then against the British as they arrived in Natal and finally between the British and Boers. I wondered how the British soldiers had felt facing the Zulu during the Zulu wars. They certainly did not get it all their own way having suffered terrible losses at a place called Isandlwana when the Zulu army overran the British, slaughtering all the soldiers.

The train stopped briefly at Ladysmith but only long enough to allow me to stretch my legs when I walked up to see the engines. Ladysmith was where the Boers and British fought a pitched battle during the Anglo-Boer War. A long siege of the town had taken place.

Walter and Taffy had developed a relationship where they argued over anything. The arguments would drag on for hours, occasionally seeming to get close to blows only to pass as quickly as they had begun. Then everything returned to normal for a while before it stated up again. Taffy was the stirrer and Walter always took the hook. I was the one who tried to stay out of it, but when push came to shove I stepped in to arbitrate. Being confined to the train compartment this bickering became wearying indeed.

The last short stretch of the journey between Pinetown and Durban was agonisingly slow. While I like train travel, I was anxious to get off. It had been a long journey from Salisbury and while the spirits of our chaps was good, mixing with the South African recruits since Johannesburg had tended to turn the overall mood aboard the train sour. It was not easy to relate to those who deliberately spoke Afrikaans rather than English. A few chaps had nearly come to blows with some Afrikaans fellows which made me wonder whose side were they really on.

The train finally pulled into the Durban station somewhere around seven in the morning. Once off the train we had to wait around for an hour before the transport trucks arrived.

Our next chapter was about to commence and one that would have a profound impact on the rest of my life.

Chapter Three

Clairwood, on the outskirts of Durban, was where they dumped us. It was an army transit camp in a grass paddock. The tents were already set up in long lines with stretcher beds inside each tent. There was a larger tent that served as the mess where we would rotate through to be fed. The camp was fenced off to keep us in as I could not think of any reason why a person would want to come into the camp.

Once settled in we all were issued with day passes. The lads were in a hurry to get to the city after being cooped up on a train for days. We had not been told how long we would be in this camp, so I decided I should get my uniforms cleaned in case we did stay awhile. I sorted through my kit, collected the clothes I wanted laundered and, together with my pals, we set off to the city by catching the bus.

The city was a real hustle and bustle of activity. I was excited to be in amongst it.

Durban was a far bigger city than any of the towns we had in Rhodesia so this was a grand experience. At that moment it was hard to imagine there was a war raging in Europe and in some parts of Africa. Other than seeing quite a few chaps in uniform, the scene was carefree and peaceful as people went about their own business.

Walter had complained endlessly about the food we had been getting on the train and wanted a good fry up. We had been given some names of places that would cater for the army chaps so he wanted to get to one of them quickly. However I wanted to get my laundry booked in first. After a short argument I got my way and we went in search of a place that did laundry. The first place we called into was the OK Bazaar. At the dry cleaning counter I was told it would cost 45 pennies for each uniform and it would take two days before collection. We were only being paid 50 pennies a day so I was shocked at that price. I hesitated but also did not want to embarrass myself by indicating I could not afford to pay for laundry. Fortunately Taffy stepped in saying we may not be here in Durban that long which gave us the excuse to leave.

Stutterfords Department Store was across the road so we went there. Upon entering the store it was obvious to me that it was a grand place and my hope of finding a cheaper laundry option here quickly faded. I suggested we should go elsewhere but Walter had seen a sign to a tea room and he wanted to go there. As we waded through a throng of people on the ground floor making our way towards the stairs that led to the tea room, Taffy spotted a sign 'Dry Cleaning' so I thought that I may as well check the prices.

At that moment I was oblivious that my life was just about to irreversibly change.

As we approached the counter I stopped dead in my tracks and stared. Serving another customer was a young woman. When she looked up and her eyes met mine I choked. Her bright eyes, lovely big smile and beautiful shining dark hair sent me into a spin in that instant.

Inexplicably my stomach tightened and I had to catch my breath. Taffy asked what was wrong but I was unable to speak for a while. I was paralysed, standing there like a sack of potatoes unable to do anything. Taffy stepped forward to ask about the cleaning prices. It was slightly cheaper so they booked in their laundry. I was unable to stop staring at this girl with the dark hair. My hands shook when I passed my laundry to her.

Walter then resumed his obsession about getting tea and cake and so the two of them both headed towards the stairs. "Come on George for God's sake!" shouted Walter which snapped me out of being transfixed. I stumbled off after them, bumping into a few people. Half way up the staircase I stumbled and had to sit down on the stairs to steady myself. It felt as if I had low blood sugar levels. The lads showed only passing concern about my wellbeing having set their mind on their stomachs. After a few minutes I made my way to the tea room to join them. I drank the tea with lots of sugar, but was unable to eat anything. Both Walter and Taffy tucked in, polishing off the lot.

All I could think about was that girl and I decided to speak to her on our way out. Coming down the stairs my heart began pounding and my palms began to sweat. I could not fathom why I was behaving like this.

Such disappointment! She was not at the counter. I searched all around before spotting her talking to a customer at another counter. The chaps pressed me to leave and so sadly I had to pass on.

The bright day light hit me like a sledge hammer as we emerged from the more dimly lit store and I walked straight into several people as the throng of humanity on the pavement engulfed us. It was the lunch time hour and the pavements were a buzz with pedestrians. I can't recall seeing anything or what the conversation was about while we made our way to the Victoria League Club to have lunch. I was transfixed on the image of that girl imprinted in my mind's eye.

Once at the Club, I felt that I could not face food because my stomach was still in a knot. I therefore didn't order any food. Sitting at the dining room table watching the other two plough through their food I remembered a saying 'Faint heart never won a fair lady' so by the time their desserts arrived I had made my mind up. I went to a payphone, looked up the telephone number for Stuttafords Department Store and rang the number. I asked the switchboard operator to put me through to the Dry Cleaning counter. The wait as she connected me was agonising. My mind raced, palms sweating again and my heart beat sped up.

I then realised that didn't know that girl's name! Nor had I looked to see if she wore a wedding or engagement ring.

Someone answered the telephone as it clicked through. I spluttered asking to speak to the dark haired girl. It was awkward as the girl on the other end of the telephone said no dark haired girl worked at that counter. I explained that we had recently been in to the store to have laundry cleaned and a dark haired girl had served us. The woman on the line finally said she knew who the person I had described was, telling me that she worked in another department in the store. She went on to explain that the person I wanted to speak with had relieved another lady earlier that morning and asked if she could help me with my query. I said not really and asked if she could fetch her to the telephone, which she did.

When this girl came on the line my throat seized momentarily. However, I managed to blurt out something to start the conversation.

"Hello. I am the Army fellow who handed you my laundry and I hope you will not be annoyed with me in what I am going to ask you. I wanted to ask you in the shop but I didn't in case you hit me or something. So I'm phoning you so that you can't. Frame is the name. George Frame. Maybe you will recall?"

"Yes I remember you", came the reply in a sweet, lovely voice.

My throat tightened again.

"Well I was wondering if you would like to go out with me to the bioscope (cinema) and dinner."

Waiting for a reply was agony. My hand that held the telephone was shaking. I wondered if this was going to be the last time I ever spoke to her.

"I am terribly sorry. I have to do something tonight. Maybe some other time?"

"How about tomorrow then," I said before she could hang up. "We could have dinner and go to a show."

"Well I really don't know…"

"Please come." I sounded desperate. That was because I was desperate. "That's of course if you are not going out."

"Well. Ring me on Monday then."

"Righty Oh. I will ring. Thanks ever so much. Goodbye. Oh what is your name?"

"Lorraine, Goodbye George."

Well I was thrilled. What a relief that was. I was happy to know she was at least a bit interested and my fear that she would be married was swept away. I had worried that surely she must be married? But if she was married then she would not have said for me to call on Monday?

When I returned to the dining room I slapped Walter so hard on his back he nearly choked on whatever he had in his mouth. I was ecstatic and ordered a meal, much to their surprise at my rapid recovery. They pressed me on what I was up to, but I decided to keep this one to myself for now. However I knew deep down the next day, Sunday, was going to be miserable. Monday could not come quick enough!

Durban. The 3 Musketeers. George on the left.

(George Frame collection)

I awoke more excited than I could recall in my entire life. I was impatient to get going into Durban and to the Victoria League Club where I could get to a phone. Walter was ready to leave but Taffy and Gordon were not, so we left them, agreeing to meet for lunch. As soon as we got outside the army barracks gate we were lucky to get a lift in a car to Durban. Once we arrived at the Victoria League Club I made straight to the phone. I found myself shaking again as I dialled the number. I was sweating. My heart was pounding in my ears.

"Are we going out?" was what I blurted out unceremoniously or that's what I meant to say.

"Oh? You're going out?" came the reply and I detected disappointment.

"No! No, not unless you come out with me."

"Oh! That's different then. Well it's okay for tonight."

The conversation is etched in my mind. It was the conversation that made the arrangement for the first date with the only woman I have ever truly loved.

At six that evening I met Lorraine outside Stuttafords. My pulse was racing, but when I saw her standing and smiling up at me with those wonderful shining eyes, I felt something drop into my shoes. I was sure it was my heart because it stopped beating.

She took me to the ANZAC tea room which I will never forget because it was to be the first meal we had together. What a meal it turned out to be. I was so nervous. I could not get the peas onto my fork, nearly chocked twice and split the water. I was very glad when the dinner ended.

I found out much later the reason she chose the ANZAC tea room. She thought I was Australian because of the slouch hat I wore. The Australians had a bad reputation in Durban and she nearly did not agree to go out with me because of this.

George with his slouch hat

(George Frame collection)

We had time to spare before the bioscope and so we decided to catch a bus ride to the beach and back. We talked all the way and I knew then that I was head over heels in love with this person. I began to hope she may fall in love with me, but felt that was going to be a long shot. She was too lovely to consider me. Besides we were soon to be off to war and I was unsure for how long that would be.

After the film was finished, which I have no idea what it was called, I walked her to a spot where her brother was waiting to take her home. It was then that I realised I still did not know her full name! She told me it was Lorraine Margaret Cordner.

I asked her if I could see her again and she said yes. I walked on air back to the bus station and at one point did a skip. That was a bad decision because I fell over and nearly broke something.

Upon arrival back at camp I found that a strong wind had swept through, demolishing many tents, including ours. Luckily my kit had not gone with the tent. We spent most of the night resurrecting tents. The next day I woke with an eager anticipation of meeting Lorraine again that evening. But at parade we were told the Rhodesians were rostered on guard duty. I was rostered on for the first shift that evening. Well I was mortified and quickly decided that the only thing to do was find a way to get out of it. I paid a lad one pound, a small fortune, to do the guard duty for me.

George's pals in Durban with a rickshaw in traditional Zulu dress

(George Frame collection)

Walter, Taffy and I set off to get to town as quickly as we could and went through the gates of the camp at 9:55 AM. As we passed through we heard the call to get back. I panicked thinking I had been caught out. Being placed on a charge would mean confinement to barracks for days. As it turned out a Sergeant admonished us for leaving before ten. He spoke to us as if we were dogs. It was to be the first of several occasions of rottenness in the Army when some of those with authority looked down on the individual soldier as if he was dirt. Walter went up to him and put his face so close to his before telling him that if he spoke to us like that again he would be talking through his bum because Walter would hit him so hard his head would come out his back side.

George in Durban – picture he gave Lorraine

(George Frame collection)

I called Lorraine on the phone before lunch time to make arrangements for the evening and she invited me for dinner at her home. I had not expected that and while it sounded delightful, I worried in case I did not make the right impression on her parents.

At six that evening I met Lorraine outside the store. Her sister was with her and together we walked to where her father was with the car. As it turned out the evening was delightful, I met all her sisters and her parents and, importantly, it looked as if her mother liked me. I thought to myself that if her mother liked me then perhaps I would stand a chance with her daughter.

Saying goodnight was hard. I did not want to go. It took all of my willpower to stop myself from trying to kiss her. I worried that I could spoil everything if I did try and she didn't want to. That night I lay awake a long time thinking of Lorraine and how all my life I had dreamt of finding such a woman. But had I found her too late? Any time soon we would be shipped off to war. I was ecstatically happy yet deeply sad and those two emotions wrestled with each other as I drifted off to sleep.

The next twenty one days were magical. I met Lorraine each day. On the forth evening we shared a long kiss and our embrace was passionate. Each evening we would meet to have dinner somewhere, talk, walk hand in hand, occasionally go to the bioscope, but always were terrifically happy to be together. Lorraine introduced me to all her family, aunts and uncles, her granny and even close family friends. I told her about my life up to this point and she relayed hers to me. It seemed as if we fitted together like a hand in a silk glove. Every moment together was precious.

I had known Lorraine for just over a week when, putting my arms around her, I whispered to her.

"Lorraine. Oh darling I love you more than I can tell you."

These were words I had never spoken to any other girl before. I meant them from deep in my soul.

"What has happened that makes this so cruel. I have found you for only such a short time."

"I feel that I am falling in love with you George," she said.

Heavens above. She loves me!

"Oh darling Lorraine," I replied holding her tightly in my arms. "To think the ship is already on its way here to take me away."

She put her finger on my lip and said, "Let's not talk about you having to go away. I'm too happy just being with you now."

Lorraine. (George Frame collection)

Unavoidably I introduced Lorraine to Walter, Gordon and Taffy and they had suggested a Sunday picnic. I would have preferred to just spend the day with Lorraine alone but Taffy insisted and mentioned it to Lorraine when we had met in the city at a café a few days earlier. She thought it would be a lovely chance to have an outing.

Well it was a disaster for me because I acted stupidly, which consequently threatened my relationship with Lorraine. Having settled down at the picnic site for a lazy morning and after having tea, the group decided to go to a nearby dance hall. I was enthusiastic about that because I liked dancing and thought it would allow me the opportunity to dance with my darling Lorraine. She did not want to go but would not explain her reason. I got into a huff and went off with the group, leaving her at the picnic site with Walter who never went dancing. I didn't enjoy the half hour that I danced with a few girls there because I was thinking about Lorraine. I went out to the balcony of the dance hall to see her talking to Walter and then on the second occasion I went out they both were gone. A huge wave of jealously came over me and irrational thoughts poured into my mind.

The picnic that nearly ended the love story before it had begun. George and Lorraine on the top right.

(George Frame collection)

When we got back to the picnic site Lorraine and Walter were still not there. My jealousy notched up irrationally so by the time they did arrive back, smiling away, I was in a foul mood. I sulked through lunch like a petulant child. At one point, watching Walter talking to her, I wanted to punch him. I succeeded in making the afternoon unpleasant and ended up going back to the army barrack alone early in the evening leaving Lorraine at the bus stop to catch her bus home. What a foolish goose I was!

We had previously arranged to meet after work on the Monday, however I was unsure if she would want to see me again. I had the whole day to stew on how stupid I had been. Thankfully she was standing at the place we had arranged to meet which was a massive relief for me, but things were tense between us. After a short while however she apologised for going off with Walter. I acted as if it had not mattered but clearly my attempt at acting reflected why I had never been attracted to the theatre as a career. Fortunately we spoke about it and the ice quickly melted so that by the end of that evening we were okay. I was so remorseful, vowing to myself to learn a sombre lesson from my bad behaviour. Lorraine could not dance, hence her reluctance to want to go to that bloody dance hall. I took it she didn't want to spend time with me. While waiting for us to come back, she had asked Walter to walk with her along the river, which I had taken for her deciding to match up with him, thinking to myself that I was really just a passing soldier that such a lovely person would pass over. How very stupid!

The idyllic times where Lorraine and I cuddled and kissed, talked and sat in quiet contemplation together was to come to a screeching end. It had to end. I knew that was going to occur, but I had tried very hard to pretend that was not going to happen. To think about leaving her to go to a war thousands of miles away had become too unbearable. I asked myself what on earth possessed me to decide to volunteer to go and fight the Germans. It was an irrational question because had I not done so I would not be here in Durban and would not have met my lovely Lorraine. I thought it so unfair how the cards had been dealt.

That Saturday morning was beautiful when I emerged from the tent having had a restful night's sleep wrapped in a dream about Lorraine. Standing on parade as we had done for the past twenty two days, we went through the same brain numbing roll call. I was thinking about how wonderful the weekend was going to be with my love when the announcement hit me like a sledge hammer to my temple.

".... At 0900 tomorrow you will be transported to the docks to board the transport ship ....."

That struck like a hammer to the skull. Had I heard that correctly, I wondered? Tomorrow we were to be transported away from this place!

Tonight was to be the last free pass and only until 10 PM.

Lorraine and I spent that last evening walking along the beach front before going back to her house. Trying not to show how devastated we both were that this time to depart had actually arrived was very hard. We hugged each other when these thoughts took over, knowing that if we looked into each other's eyes at those moments we would both cry. We tried to capture all the love that was ours and which we knew belonged to us in those last few precious hours.

The parting was bitter and it wrenched a part of my heart out. I could not bear looking down into those gorgeous eyes that welled up with tears. Oh how I wanted to cry out in despair!

I walked down the hill from Lorraine's house to the bus stop soaked in immense sadness. And an anger welled up inside me that I had not expected. Bugger the world and its unfairness I thought, before my mind went numb.

Chapter Four

July 1941

I awoke depressed that Sunday.

The freshness and beauty of the morning that usually greeted me was gone, replaced by a sense that my world was about to come crashing down around me. The sound of the trucks arriving heralded in the reality of it and when they pulled into the camp to take us to the dock I gave up hope that today was not happening. I realised that I was really quite angry at the world.

We were crammed in the back of the truck like sardines. As I was somewhere in the middle and therefore because the truck had a canvas cover I was unable to see out as we drove along. My misguided hope to catch a glimpse of Lorraine one last time before we boarded the ship was never going to happen.

Up until the minute I stepped onto the concrete of the dock I had not given any thought as to what the ship would be like, nor had I really grasped the dangers that existed in being transported by troop ship during a war. While we were driving along the conversation among some of the chaps hinged on speculation about the ship, its size and what the accommodation would be like. Walter asked me for my opinion and I snapped back "Who the bloody hell cares."

At the dock we had to line up in rows. The roll call was made and when all were accounted for, we then had to march along the dock to board the ship. Hell what a size the ship was! I had never seen anything as big before. When we passed the bow heading towards the boarding plank I noticed the name. Mauretania. I recalled this was a famous Cunard Line ship. How fortunate we were to be going on this ship I thought to myself. But then we kept marching past.

The next ship along the wharf was called the Nieuw Amsterdam. It was a fine looking two funnelled ship, painted in a dull grey. I later found out it had only recently been built and was the flagship of the Holland America Line, called the 'Darling of the Dutch". This was the ship we were going to board and I took an immediate dislike to it. It was the vessel that was about to tear me away from my darling Lorraine.

It took a long time for us to board because we each had to be identified and given our billet information. I was allocated a cabin down below just above the water line. At least it had a porthole. The cabin was stripped bare other than hammocks strung up and not at all like what I had deluded myself to expect. Because I had never slept in a hammock before and I did not know what to anticipate, I selected the lower one.

What a miserable morning it was when I rolled out of my hammock after spending the worst night I had ever had since leaving home. Sleeping in a hammock for the first time was no joke as every time I rolled over I fell out. To make it worse, the cabin was as hot as Hades, the chaps in the cabin were sweating and farting so by morning the smell was awful. I thought to myself that being down in this place must be like being in the Black Hole of Calcutta.

I dressed quickly and rushed up to the deck hoping we would get shore leave, but was bitterly disappointed to discover no shore leave was posted. My heart sank to the bottom of my boots. Breakfast was served in the second class dining room, which I really had no appetite for, before a parade up on deck that was a total waste of time and effort. While standing to attention on the deck the realisation that I was not going to see my Lorraine again before we left overwhelmed me. When we were dismissed from parade I was feeling emotionally worse than I could ever recall. It had not crossed my mind that we would not get a pass for shore leave, given the damn ship was not leaving until later in the afternoon.

I kept going back to the notice board in the desperate hope the shore leave would be posted, but nothing changed. If only I could get ashore to a phone and hear her voice and tell her once again how madly in love I was with her. But I was not able to see a way to get one foot off the damn ship other than jumping overboard.

After lunch I walked the deck like a caged animal, staring out to the city. At around four in the afternoon I noticed that smoke began to billow from the ship's funnels and soon thereafter saw the tugs moving in towards the ship. This sealed our fate to the oceans as the ship was soon away from the dockside and being turned around by the tugs to face the Bluff and beyond that the Indian Ocean.

The funnel whistle blew a few times and, as I stood watching the crowd of people who had assembled to wave the ship away, the pain in my heart was just about killing me. I had never experienced any emotion like that before. A terrible big lump came into my throat and I nearly broke out crying. I had to fight that back because the chaps around me would really have rubbed it in forever thinking I was either crying because I was going away from Mummy or going to a war.

I walked aimlessly around the deck watching the Bluff pass us by when the ship moved out of the harbour. Before long the sun began to set and with it my spirits sank even lower with the land fading in the distance. I began to live for the day when I would be on my way back to her. I missed dinner and it was around midnight when I said goodbye to my darling and finally made my way back down to the cabin. I did not sleep well.

The next day saw the ship battling a large swell with no land in sight. None of my group of pals were sick but I noticed others were, many looking quite green.

We had parade followed by a boat drill. I wondered why they left boat drill until after we were well out to sea rather than yesterday when we sat in the harbour most of the day. At the parade we were informed that we were being transported to Egypt.

I was very hungry so was ready for breakfast. After that I went out on deck and off to port noticed a superb sleek looking war ship which I thought must be our escort. On the starboard side was the Mauretania who must have caught up overnight. I was fascinated to watch the escort as it moved ahead then slowed down, before passing behind us to come up again on the other side, like a sheep dog minding a heard of sheep. A few ships passed us going in the opposite direction and whenever another ship appeared the escort would shoot off to investigate.

The escorts that guarded us en-route to Egypt

(George Frame collection)

The Mauretania sailing en-route to Egypt

(George Frame collection)

I spent most of my time while aboard with Walter and Taffy who chose to mock me for being like a love sick puppy. How observant they were! We began to talk more about the adventure that we were heading to speculating on what wonders we would get to see. I wanted to see the Pyramids and the Sphinx. We joked how we were going to teach the Germans a lesson, wondering what section of the Army we would end up in and what gun we would be issued with, each hoping for a Bren gun.

I had shot many animals in the bush back in Rhodesia. Antelope and bush pigs, mainly for rations. Taffy had shot birds and Walter had shot nothing. I was therefore more experienced in killing animals and knew what damage a bullet could do as it tore through muscle and bone. I had also seen a dead person. The others had not yet experienced that. When I worked on the mines in Northern Rhodesia overhead power lines had fallen down and a black African mine worker had been electrocuted. His colleagues had run to tell me and I went with them to investigate. At the scene the poor fellow lay dead. I asked the colleagues how the accident had occurred. One black African leapt forward to tell me that his colleague had picked up the wire. He then bent down to show me and before I knew it he picked up the electrical wire and was electrocuted himself. The smell of burning flesh stayed with me for a long time. I also witnessed injuries of limbs being severed in the mine, with blood squirting everywhere. I felt I knew what to expect in the war and explained this picture to the others, but I doubt it sank in.

Each day, with monotonous regularity, we had morning parade. The rest of the day was to our own. Those on charges would have tasks allocated like cleaning toilets and swabbing decks. Because they needed these tasks done, the opportunity to get placed on a charge was high. My goal was to avoid that opportunity.

Staring at the ocean was mesmerising. I recalled how I used to look at the ocean for long periods when, as a young boy on my way to boarding school in Britain, I was alone with my brothers aboard a ship.

On this voyage I didn't really think too much about being torpedoed. I believed that the Germans were unlikely to have submarines on the east coast of Africa. Someone suggested it was the Japanese submarines that we had to watch for but that too seemed farfetched because I didn't think we were at war with Japan. We had all been told that while on deck to keep an eye out for anything unusual like a submarine or a torpedo. Not many of us did that though. I had never seen either a submarine or a torpedo before so was unsure what they looked like.

The ship was in blackout during the night, so when on deck it was dark. Each night I lay on my back on the deck staring at the sky with its billions of stars. The stars shone so brightly and they reminded me of Lorraine's eyes that I had fallen in love with. I decided to write to her and ask her to marry me and so the next day I spent ages constructing the sentences. After many attempts I finally got it right and feeling exuberant I posted the letter at the Pursers Office.

On the third day one of our crowd made a wonderful discovery. A swimming pool on a few decks below. We spent an hour in the water and it was delightful. The chaps were all sworn not to spread the word to others. We did not want too many to know, nor did we want the captain to shut off access.

As we made our way northwards it was too hot to try and sleep in our cabin so the three of us packed our things and went in search of a sleeping place on deck. We found a spot on the front of the top deck. I was relieved because there was a cool breeze from the forward motion of the ship. I had a sleeping bag that I had brought with me from Rhodesia. It was very handy indeed. Walter laughed whenever I was trying to get in or out of the sleeping bag remarking that I would never be able to get out of it quick enough when enemy planes came over. That didn't worry me at the time as my main concern was to get some shut eye.

One evening Walter had an altercation with one of the Imperial Officers who had spoken to him as if he was dirt. The stuck up sod was so arrogant talking as if he had an apple stuck up his ass. Walter told him to get the hell out of his sight before he threw the bastard overboard. The Officer backed off pretty quickly. We thought Walter would be placed on a charge of insubordination so we scarpered from the spot that incident took place. Because it was dark on deck we hoped the bastard didn't see any distinguishing markings or the detail of Walter's face. As it turned out after some unnecessary anxiety, nothing happened.

We heard that a soldier had died aboard and he was to be buried at sea. We stood on deck to watch as his body, wrapped in cloth, slipped out from under the Union Jack and fell into the ocean.

The days turned to night and back to day. We used our 'exclusive' swimming pool each day. There were films showing in the theatre which were not that good, but it passed the time. A boxing tournament was held with several chaps beating the stuffing out of each other. It relieved some tension that they probably had. It was not my cup of tea though. The meals were okay. Walking around the deck could only occupy one for so long before it became meaningless.

Another parade before we discovered to our dismay that the swimming pool was packed with chaps. It was bound to happen that someone had let the cat out of the bag and our exclusive swimming pool was no more.

When I was on deck in the mid-afternoon, one of the two escort destroyers blasted its whistle several times and sped off in a zig zag fashion, its two funnels billowing out thick black smoke. This caused much interest and of course much speculation. Most chaps were then drawn to search the ocean for anything that resembled a submarine, not that many, if any, had ever seen one before. Soon thereafter the second escort replicated this as it swung away towards the Mauretania. After an hour or so the escorts returned and everything settled back into normality. We never heard what that incident was about.

Then when I woke up one day there was land to our south and we guessed it must be Italian Somaliland. I was not sure if it was still in Italian hands or whether they had been chased out. That day was hot and I fell asleep on deck while reading a book. I missed lunch as a consequence which was unfortunate because by mid-afternoon I was famished. All the contents in the food parcel Lorraine had given me the night before we boarded were gone.

The one day, after dinner, the ship turned to port which I suspected was towards the Bay of Aden. We saw a light house flashing and after watching it for some time we decided to turn in for the night.

When I woke at dawn it was already as hot as Hades. We spent that day doing very little other than sweltering on deck and drinking lemonade. Below deck it was like a furnace. The ship was in the Red Sea which was like glass. There was no wind at all. Thoughts of how lovely it would be to jump in the sea for a swim were immediately discarded when we saw large sharks in the ocean. They were following the ship, being attracted to the food scraps that were thrown overboard.

Walter woke me the next morning and I could have punched him on the nose. I was having a marvellous dream about Lorraine. After breakfast the Mauretania shot past us going like a bat out of hell before the two escorts blew whistles and turned away presumably heading back to the Indian Ocean. I thought we must now be close to our destination and, while relived that the boredom from being on the ship would be coming to an end, the prospect of soon being engaged in a war began to take presence of mind.

Our escort in the Red Sea seen through a porthole.

(George Frame collection)

A light shower of rain on that last evening did not persuade us to retreat back to the cabin. When we awoke the ship was anchored. The land around us was desolate. Just sand everywhere. There were other ships anchored in the bay aside from the two troop carriers. Two ships with USA flags, two tankers and a few cargo ships. There was a terrific looking navy ship near us presumably to give some anti-aircraft gun protection. There were also ships that had been sunk. One was ablaze in the distance. We were told it had been hit by German bombs. The smoke coming from a capsized ship looked so sad, bringing the reality that we were now in a war zone that much closer. (I later discovered it was the Georgic which had been bombed by German planes a few days earlier.)

Georgic after being bombed by the German air force in Port Tewfik

(George Frame collection)

Did you know?

The last ship ever to be built for the White Star Line, Georgic was launched on 21 November 1931 and after fit-out and sea trials, was sent to Liverpool on 12 June 1932 for her maiden voyage.

The ship was requisitioned for use as a troop carrier and was converted in Clydebank to carry over 3,000 men.

This service as a troop carrier continued successfully until 14 July 1941 when, near Port Tewfik, Georgic was bombed by the Luftwaffe.

The badly damaged ship, now beached and burnt out, was salvaged in October 1941 and sent to Port Sudan where temporary repairs were carried out.

In March 1942 Georgic was towed to Karachi for further repairs and after these repairs, Georgic sailed for Britain to be extensively rebuilt and returned as a troop carrier.

After the war she was reconfigured to be used for the Australian and New Zealand immigration service.

She was once again called into trooping service, this time for the Korean War.

Georgic was then chartered to the Australian Government as part of the "Assisted Passage" scheme, a service she remained on until November 1955.

Finally retired for good, after a brief period in lay up the last White Star Liner ever built was scrapped.

Extract from www.chriscunard.com

Our gang drew the short straw to be seconded to fetch the mail bags up from the ship's hold to be loaded onto a small ship that had come alongside. I didn't realise that mail bags could be so damn heavy. It was terribly hot and hauling the bags up from the bowels of the ship exhausted us. I wondered which bag had my letter for Lorraine proposing marriage, but then realised it would not be in these bags as the letter needed to get back to Durban. It would stay on the ship as it was going back to Durban and I hoped it would get back safely.

Port Tewfik was the port where we were to disembark. I had thought of this place as being quite romantic, being at the start of the Suez Canal, but in reality it was a desolate place full of sand and so damn hot.

Port Tewfik – the casualties of aerial bombing by the Germans.

(George Frame collection)

A great hum developed amongst the soldiers on deck when the order was given to disembark. Having spent endless boring days and nights on the ship the thought of getting off it was welcomed. It meant however that we were one step nearer to being in the war. That was what we had signed up for. To fight the Germans and deal them and their trumped up Corporal Hitler a telling blow. A few months, six months at the most, and we would have done our job was the general census of opinion.

However I was even less enthusiastic at the prospect of going to this war than I was many weeks ago. I was missing Lorraine so much and thought of her nearly all the time.

Whilst on deck I had written a poem for my Lorraine. It was now in one of the post bags. I hoped she would get it soon and remember me always as I ventured on this next journey.

To a Women Left Behind

If sometimes in the silence of the night
Your eyes are filled with aching tears
If sometimes its emptiness you see
Within the coming lonely years
And if it feels as if your heart will break
With hopeless yearning pain and fear
Remember then the day will come
When you and I will meet again

If sometimes fear should fill your soul
Because I am in a battle zone
If you should feel what I endure
Remember dearest, you're not alone
And if within a foreign land
I am within the fallen too
Remember dearest in another world
Your broken dreams will all come true

George
1941

Chapter Five

It took us ages for us to get off the ship as they worked the disembarkation from the top decks down. I wondered what fool was in charge to have made this decision given those in the lower decks were far hotter than those in the top decks.

Once off the ship we were lined up in the piercing hot sun on the dock side to be accounted for. I guessed they were not that keen to leave anyone behind. After that and having stood in the sun for an awfully long time, we were marched off to trucks for transport to a desolate sandy camp site with multiple rows of tents each bedding eight. The first order of business was that we were shown what to do in the event of an air raid and where to find our slit trench because it was expected that the Germans would attack the camp. Having seen the burning ships and with this new information it was sinking in that we were now in the war.

At the start of the following day we got a brief outline of what was happening at the front. My first impression as the briefing started was that we had come all this way for nothing because the Italians had been whipped. That immediately raised my spirits because that meant we would not be here that long and therefore I would be seeing Lorraine sooner than expected. But, as the briefing continued, I got the message that the Germans had pushed the Eighth Army back to the Egyptian border and Tobruk was still under siege. That didn't sound promising at all.

The arduous procession of morning parades followed listless nights where it was proving hard to sleep due to the heat. Each day, for a few weeks, we underwent training. We started the day with fitness training, then on to the firing range with .303 rifles, before mock bayonet charges, stabbing bags filled with sand. We had to yell as we ran towards the bags and then to stab them with ferocity. If anyone did not show enough anger when stabbing the sand bag we all had to do it again. I thought at times that the anger against some of the chaps who failed the yelling and anger aspect, which made us all redo the charges in the bloody heat, was greater than for the bags we had to stab. Running with fixed bayonets yelling at the top of one's voice was rather comical actually. The instructor told us that by yelling it would distract and frighten the enemy. I was unconvinced. I once had a buffalo charge at me bellowing like crazy and what that did for me was to focus my shot to its head, dropping it at thirty yards.

Spending hours in openly exposed semi circles under the hot sun firing machine guns at a fictitious enemy made me worry that we would be obliterated by any advancing armoured army.

Due to my time roaming the Rhodesian bush hunting for wild game I was a good marksman which seemed to impress the instructor. By comparison to some, I was a world champion marksman. I made a mental note not to get ahead of those chaps who proved to be poor shots because they would more than likely shoot me in the back.

Training to halt Rommel from taking Egypt. (George Frame collection)

I do not know how the splits were made when they allocated us to different divisions. Walter, Taffy and I were allotted to anti-tank guns. Like with artillery guns, I thought those that operated them should have at least some trigonometry knowledge to work the angles and distance calculations. Walter was good at that stuff, but I was hopeless at it when at school. I never completed high school anyway, being far too distracted by the lure of the wide open bush. However, I was glad the three of us were still together and later that week we were told we would be deployed on the same gun.

Those in the Rhodesian Regiment allotted to anti-tank gunnery were billeted together so we had to pack up our tent to relocate. I was disappointed to learn we were to be attached to the British Army and not the South African Army group. That meant we ended up with Pommy officers, many of whom we soon gathered looked down on us 'colonialists'. Walter hoped we would not get the stuck up poncy officer he had the run in with on the ship. We didn't.

It was exciting to be introduced to the anti-tank guns and their trucks. The anti-tank guns were 2 pounders with a truck and each group of three anti-tank guns had a supply truck attached to them.

For a few weeks we undertook practice on the guns which was far better than what we had been doing previously. I ended up being the chap to load the shells in the barrel and also I was to drive the supply truck. Walter was the anti-tank gun aimer, while Taffy stacked the shells and assisted moving the gun around. We had a British corporal in charge and the CO of our unit was also British.

We became quite good at firing the anti-tank gun, hitting the targets more often than not. We learned offensive tactics, how to defend ourselves if tanks and or infantry attacked and importantly what not to do in order to stay alive. We had two chaps with Bren guns to shoot at enemy infantry that may advance on our position. It was pretty obvious that if a tank came at us and we did not hit it with the first shot then we would be done for. Accuracy and speed seemed to be the two most important attributes required to stay alive, aside from a great pile of luck.

While there were some changes in other groups, with a few chaps being reallocated to infantry, our group stayed intact at the end. I was pleased with where I found myself, amongst pals and with other Rhodesians.

When we finished our training we got the news that we would be joining the 7th Armoured Division. We had no idea what the 7th Armoured Division was other than, by its title, it must have tanks and we suspected artillery. Plus anti-tank guns obviously.

The 7th Armoured Division was broken down in several sections. We were deployed to XXX Corps. The chaps figured that it was called XXX because they had run out of names, others figured it was Roman numerals for 30th Corps. Then there was further sub-groups such as the 22nd Armoured Brigade, the 4th Armoured Brigade and the South African Reconnaissance Regiment. There was a Long Range Desert Group that had Rhodesians in it and which had a reputation for having done good work in harassing the Italian and German forces and where they had blown up a large number of enemy planes in hit and run attacks.

When we all got two days leave pass the three of us caught a train into Cairo where we thought we would spend our leave. I wanted to see the Pyramids, ride a camel and see the places which I had heard exotic stories about.

Train from Port Tewfik to Cairo and Suez Canal. (George Frame collection)

Well, how disappointed was I? At each train stop more people got on and when the carriages were full they started to hang off the sides and clamber onto the roof. The whole train was packed with humanity, their baggage, chickens and goats. It was chaotic. These sweaty people, many of whom had foul body odour, talked loudly and incessantly.

As we trundled along and looking out of the train window, which I had put down to try and get some fresh air, all I could see was desert. I wondered to myself if I would ever get out of this God forsaken place.

We did get to see the Suez Canal along the route. An amazing feat of engineering undertaken by the French which had transformed sea travel between Europe and the Far East.

Young Egyptian woman minding her buffalo. (George Frame collection)

When we did get off the train we were immediately surrounded by hordes of people begging, like flies to a dead carcass. And that was pretty much what we had to endure the whole time we were in Cairo, constant begging. The station that once was grand was now old and dirty filled with vendors selling anything. We had not gone that far and already we were offered watches, daughters, boot laces, shoe shines, chickens, and introductions to prostitutes, doctors and even a dentist! As we departed the train station the first thing that struck me was the filth everywhere, followed by the smell of the place. The place was overcrowded with people. I had never seen so many people in one place before. I soon felt claustrophobic and a desire to get out of the City.

Left: Window shopping in Cairo. Right: Beggars and merchants harassed the soldiers wherever they went in Cairo. (George Frame collection)

Street scene in Cairo. (George Frame collection)

Cairo. (George Frame collection)

As we meandered through the streets I could not figure out how these Egyptians knew my name. Everywhere we went they would yell out "George!" Then it dawned on us that they called all soldiers "George", apparently after King George VI.

We went to see the Pyramids and the Sphinx. The Kings Tomb was awe inspiring with blocks of stone ten foot long fitting so precisely together. How such massive boulders were moved from quarries somewhere up the Nile River to this place with no mechanised equipment to help them was amazing. To think that five thousand years ago the Egyptians built these massive structures, yet today they lived so chaotically confounded me.

The Sphinx was fascinating. I had been told that Napoleon was to blame for the facial disfigurement of the Sphinx. If that was true, why Napoleon thought it clever or masculine to have a cannon shoot at its head is beyond belief. To see such an ancient structure desecrated was sad.

The pyramids and the Sphynx were an awe inspiring experience.

(George Frame collection)

George found it fascinating how the ancient Egyptians could have built these large
structures by bringing huge stone slabs from many hundreds of miles away.
(George Frame collection)

I wanted to ride a camel thinking it would be a wonderful experience.
When we got to where the camel ride vendors were located, all hell broke
out as the vendors squabbled amongst themselves while inundating us with
offers. I soon discovered that the Camels stank badly, were uncomfortable
to ride and after the ride I wished I had not bothered.

George with a camel and its minder. The experience was forgettable

(George Frame collection)

Post card from Cairo to Lorraine. Lorraine with her parents as a back drop to George in Egypt

(George Frame collection)

We were told that the New Zealand Club in Cairo was a good place to go for a meal, so late in the afternoon we made our way there. We were welcomed once we convinced them we were not Australian. We wore slouch hats which looked very much like the Australian army hats so we had some convincing to do. We eagerly drank beer, tucked in to a good hearty meal while making acquaintances with several blokes who told us stories of what they had been through. It sounded dreadful.

Some Rhodesians enjoying a pint of beer (or more) in a Serviceman's club in Cairo. George on the right.

(George Frame collection)

Did you know?

Operation Battleaxe occurred in June 1941. Its prime objective was to relieve the siege of Tobruk and push the German and Italian armies out of eastern Cyrenaica in Libya. The operation failed as the German defence was held and the British lost over half of their tanks in the first day.

Just shy of 1,000 British and Commonwealth soldiers were killed against less than 700 Axis soldiers, but the British lost around 100 tanks and 36 aircraft to 12 Axis tanks and 10 aircraft.

Later that evening we made our way, or should I suggest, we staggered, to the digs we had found through the advice of the New Zealand chaps which were relatively clean and not that expensive. With the black out it was not easy to navigate around the narrow and winding streets but luckily there was a full moon that helped a lot. When we turned a corner we were confronted by two local women who propositioned us by lifting their clothes so we could inspect the goods. I was shocked, while Taffy wanted to have a closer look, we grabbed him and hurried away.

The ladies of the night operated day and night trying to solicit trade from the soldiers

(George Frame collection)

Returning to camp after our leave, we had to pack up straight away to board the train back to Cairo where we were transported by trucks to our new camp about ten miles out of Cairo. The tents at the new camp were half underground which made sense. If the camp was bombed, unless you were standing, the shrapnel would not hit you, as long as the bomb did not directly hit the tent that is.

At our first parade in this new location, the camp CO said that he welcomed the Rhodesians who had volunteered to help the Empire fight the war. All 60 of us! We were given leave until midnight and so we made haste to get a tram to Cairo with the intent of going back to the New Zealand Club. The tram was packed to over flowing. When we got to the Club we tucked into a meal of eggs, tomato and chips, with beer to wash it down. We discovered that some of our New Zealand buddies had been shipped off back to the front that day.

We were attested into the British Eighth Army the next day and had to swear an oath of allegiance to King and Country. After that we were issued with British uniforms, kit and importantly new pay books. The British were paid more than we had been paid so we felt that was a positive to compensate having Pommy Officers in charge.

Eighth Army Formation Badge

Life in the camp soon became boring. There was no action in sight and the days were filled with the early morning parade and cleaning kit. We did however get passes each evening, time well spent at the New Zealand Club.

The three musketeers. George in the middle. (George Frame collection)

One day Peter, who was in our crew, said he had had enough of parades and would not attend them again. We told him he would be put on detention and would have to clean the toilets. He thought about that for a few moments before deciding on a plan to let it be known he has unwell and then faint so he could be taken off the parade ground. The next day he faked his faint and while he was being pulled off with his feet dragging behind him the Warrant Officer shouted "pick up your damned feet soldier," whereupon Peter made the mistake, even though momentarily, of moving his legs. He got detention and toilet cleaning duties for a week and still had to attend the parades as well.

I was summoned to the CO who told me, that as a designated driver, I was to go on vehicle servicing training. I already knew how to service a vehicle but thought this new order would at least get me out of the camp. The training was to be done at a large warehouse type facility nearer to Cairo. I was there over several weeks where I learned nothing that new on servicing trucks. I was however able to inspect many tanks that were being repaired, some badly damaged, which made the experience useful seeing many of us were yet to actually see a tank up close. The tanks being repaired were mostly Cruiser tanks and were far bigger than I had imagined them to be. Yet they were still very cramped inside. At six foot three inches I struggled to fit in anywhere. Some Matilda tanks arrived for engine services and they were more impressive looking. Knowing that we would be shooting at these monsters soon, albeit German or Italian models, and seeing what armament they could fire back at us, was sobering indeed.

This particular evening had started as all others had. We were getting ready to fetch the leave passes when the sirens went off. This set of a mini panic as chaps scrambled to get cover in the slit trenches or anywhere that looked safe. I got into a slit trench and waited. When I heard the drone of the planes it sounded ominous. Then the anti-aircraft guns blasted away amongst the thud, thud of bombs exploding in the distance. When I peered over the edge of the trench I saw the multitude of search lights that lit up the sky. Very impressive indeed to see the search lights, AA gun explosions in the sky and the sound of it all going off.

When the Luftwaffe came overhead, the night shy lit up with search lights and anti-aircraft gun fire

(George Frame collection)

The news that our army was making a push west and that we were soon to join the action brought with it mixed emotions and different sensations. Following the many months of monotony in the camps, the prospect of actually doing something, other than parades, cleaning kit and being told about basic mechanics, was an invigorating thought. We had come all this way to fight the Germans and Italians to stop them from their quest to dominate the world, so now the prospect of actually seeing action would fulfil that objective. Being able to shoot our guns in anger rather than at targets was going to be exciting. However, recalling the stories told to us by the New Zealand chaps regarding the brutality of the fighting dampened the enthusiasm of engaging in the fighting somewhat. It certainly did not sound like a walk in the park, especially when fighting the Nazi. I certainly had some mixed emotions. I was as keen as ever to get through whatever there was ahead of us as quickly as possible so that I could get back to my darling Lorraine. The thought of never seeing her again was tearing at my heart strings each day but now the reality of us going to face the enemy and shoot at each other meant I may actually may not make it back.

We were transported to another camp at Heliopolis to be equipped with our anti-tank guns, trucks, ordinances and other supplies. The equipment was all brand new. I felt proud to start the engine of my truck.

We were set up as self-contained units in the reserve force with the prime objective to defend the chaps in the front line whenever any enemy tanks broke through so they could not be outflanked. We would also be roaming and attacking any enemy stragglers.

Writing home from a camp site in the dessert in the hope the letters would be delivered.

(George Frame collection)

It helped mentally and emotionally to get a clearer idea of what we would be doing. For me being in reserve and not in the front line was encouraging for the prospect of getting home in one piece one day. Nonetheless shooting at tanks was always going to be a high risk activity as we would soon discover.

Chapter Six

It was early on a sunny morning when the convoy pulled out of the camp at Heliopolis. Our destination was Mersa Matruh situated on the Mediterranean coast and our route took us along the sealed coastal road.

That first night out in the desert was terrible. It was bloody cold. Introduced to hordes of sand fleas, I decided to lie on the tarmac to get away from them and managed to get a few hours' sleep. At day break it dawned on me how stupid I had been because a convoy could have come along during the night and run over me.

On the road moving west towards Mersa Matruth. (George Frame collection)

When we arrived at Mersa Matruh I am not sure what I was expecting. It was underwhelming except the sea looked inviting. Some chaps ran off to have a swim while we waited for orders on what we were to do next. Without much persuasion I joined in. The water was glorious. We were naked, splashing around having a good time of it when the CO yelled at us to get out. The word was that the beach had been mined and only a few days before a South African soldier had been blown to bits near where we were. We all carefully walked back across the beach following the foot prints we had made when we rushed down to the sea.

Our camp set up near the beach. (George Frame collection)

The bulk of the convoy moved off towards the west but our orders were to stay there which suited us fine. We set up camp under the palm trees and settled in. But that was short lived. Within a few days we were ordered to move west and take up a rear guard position near what was called Hell Fire Pass, which sounded like it was not a great place to be. It actually was called Helfaya Pass, an escarpment of some 600 feet with a windy road that passed a few miles inland from the sea allowing transit between Egypt and Libya. Whoever controlled that pass really controlled the way in and out of Egypt along the coastal strip. Therefore it was a strategic transport route which the Germans now held.

Once we got close to the Pass we found a slightly elevated location where the road twisted on a long curve. That was where we dug in the anti-tank guns. We were able to see anything advancing eastwards and we would be able to get in a shot before the enemy could see us. That was the theory.

Once our gun was in position we went looking around on foot to familiarise ourselves with what was there. We came across a ruin of a building that was close to where we were. It had no roof, only broken down walls. We figured that the bits of wall could protected us from the wind and sand being blown around so we set up our sleeping arrangements there by hanging a tarpaulin overhead and clearing some rocks away. The next night Fred fell asleep with his cigarette alight which set fire to his bedding. He got away with only superficial burns, but we lost the tarpaulin and other bedding including, my sleeping bag.

Lost my sleeping bag. (George Frame collection)

We didn't stay at that location for very long. We received orders to transit over rough country to the south of the Pass to join up with the XXX Corps further west.

It was in mid-November 1941 when Operation Crusader kicked off. I understood at that time it was to be the push against Rommel to relieve the siege at Tobruk.

We had passed through Sidi Omar and were heading westwards following the 7th Armoured Division into the expanse of desert moving towards Gabr Saleh. We were told to expect a tank battle to occur at this location. We were to remain in reserve behind the battle lines. The feeling amongst the chaps was one of mixed emotions. Keenness to get into the war after all the preparation, yet, for some of us, anxiety as to what to expect.

A large convoy of tanks passed by where we had been holding up. The cloud of dust was enormous and that made me wonder how the aspect of any surprise attack could ever be achieved in the desert. They were heading to Gabr Saleh, a place, it turned out, of no inspiration at all.

Nothing much appeared to happen that day which led to some disappointment amongst the chaps in general.

The next day news filtered in that the 1st South African Division and the 22nd Armoured Brigade who were further to the west had been engaged in fierce fighting against the Italians at a place called Bir el Gubi and that they had not come off that well. This news was confusing as we understood the Italians had been beaten and were not that impressive in the field. We therefore suspected the Germans were there and had been the force that inflicted the damage.

We then began to move northwards trailing behind the main force.

A big battle took place north of our location when our chaps took Sidi Rezegh which was a strategic airfield that the Germans had in the middle of nowhere.

At this stage we had done a lot of driving but as yet we were yet to see the enemy. The only enemies I had experienced were the bloody flies that pestered us constantly and the sand storms that drove sand everywhere, into the eyes, nose, ears, mouth, food, the bedding, the cab of the truck; you name it and there would be sand.

However, my war was about to begin in earnest.

On the move in pursuit of the Italians – 2 pounder anti-tank gun

(George Frame Collection)

No one could be prepared for the sight that confronted us when we arrived at the location where a battle had been only the day before. It was truly horrible. The picture in front of us was really grim. Burned out tanks, trucks and guns were scattered all over the place. I was shocked, stunned actually and I was not alone in that feeling.

We stopped to have a look around at a particular group of burned out tanks as the CO was interested to see what the tanks looked like. The stench of burned and rotting flesh lingered. Some chaps gagged and a few even vomited. We wandered around, somewhat dazed, looking at this sad human tragedy when suddenly we were fired at. Puffs of sand erupted near us and the ricochet of bullets hitting some of the tanks were the first we became aware of it.

Being green horns we all stood around wondering what was happening and we were lucky not to have been hit before the CO shouted at us to take cover. He indicated that the firing was coming from a low rocky outcrop. I scampered off behind a burned out truck and lay down on the ground. It was obvious that whoever was shooting was not playing games. After a while the shooting stopped and we slowly and cautiously emerged from the various hiding places. The CO ordered us to get to our trucks and move away quickly, which we did without hesitation. In the distance we could see some dust rising up which we suspected was the enemy making their own getaway.

Did you know?

The German Panzer had gained a formidable reputation.

The Panzer III was composed of four sections – a hull, turret, and front superstructure and an engine deck. Each section was welded and all four were bolted together. The hull was divided into two main compartments divided by a bulkhead. The front compartment held the gearbox and steering mechanism while the rear compartment housed both the fighting and engine compartment. Daimler-Benz and Henschel were the main manufacturers.

The G variant was the main one used in North Africa. Some of these were armed with 37mm guns while most had 50mm guns mounted. Both the 37mm and 50mm tanks had additional two MG 34 machine guns, one in the turret and other in the hull.

Armour protection for these tanks ranged from 21mm to 30mm.

The tanks sent to North Africa were equipped with additional air filters and different cooling fan reduction ratios to suit the harsh conditions and help prevent engine air intake problems.

Salvage operations. (George Frame collection)

Later that day we saw tanks that could be salvaged were being collected.

The 4th Armoured Brigade, which had been on the left flank of the advance and at one point was located near us, engaged the Germans in a big tank battle at Gabr Saleh. At that time we were in between Gabr Saleh and Sidi Rezegh and were ordered to turn back to Gabr Saleh to render anti-tank support.

By mid-morning we could hear the noise of the battle that was taking place over the horizon and we even saw a dog fight between Messerschmitt's and Hurricanes in the distance. I felt pity for those poor chaps involved in the battle, many of whom I knew would be killed that day. We did not get to where the battle was because orders came to hold position. We found out later that many of our tanks were knocked out.

The aftermath of a dog fight. (George Frame collection)

It was early in the morning when we stopped to brew our tea. We had broken the night's camp before dawn and set off for an hour or so before stopping. It was the practice to be awake and on the move before dawn. We had been told that it was not a good idea to linger at the spot where we stopped for the night in case the Germans had spotted the location. Staying there in that case would mean a pounding by artillery guns or a tank led assault.

I was starving and impatient for the chap who was our cook to get the meal ready, not that I expected anything better than what he had served up before. The food was monotonous and tasteless. The tea was not much better but at least it was wet and hot. I always tried to load sugar into the mug as that helped to make it taste like something you could drink at least.

Close by where we had stopped that morning was a downed Italian plane which we went to see. Another one was further along the track which was largely intact except it had no wings attached.

Downed Italian plane and Italian plane without its wings.

(George Frame collection)

Several Matilda tanks passed us, belting along, heading west. While I had seen these types of tanks before, I was still struck by their size. They certainly made a racket puffing out black smoke from their exhausts. As they passed we all gave them the 'V' for victory signs and plenty of cheers. Following them were the trucks carrying fuel supplies and given the size of the engines I had seen back in the training camp, I could understand how they guzzled fuel.

After we had stopped for a brew on one particular day, I was not paying much attention when some chaps began wandering away from the vehicles peering skywards. After a few moments I heard the droning sound. It took a while to register with me that the sound was from a plane and once it did register, I too searched the sky. The sky was not clear blue, rather it was hazy making it hard to really see in the distance. I don't recall hearing the warning shout but when the chaps began to run in all directions I gathered the situation had deteriorated to unsafe. Taffy shot past me in a sprint shouting that it was a plane and I had better get to cover. Get cover? Seriously? In the middle of a desert with no vegetation! I dropped my mug, tin plate and the spoon and belted after him not knowing where we were going. All around was flat desert. I don't think at that time I felt frightened, rather it was strangely exhilarating.

I heard the awful whining sound before Taffy, who was well ahead of me, stopped to look up. I did the same and that's when I saw the planes. They were diving straight down and making a terrible sound. It was actually fascinating to watch. The noise of guns firing filled the air as our chaps began shooting at the planes. What a commotion it was. Suddenly a huge explosion erupted as a bomb from a plane hit one of our trucks. That shook me out of the trance I was in and I turned and ran flat out towards a shallow ditch I could see twenty or so yards ahead.

I was preparing to dive for the ditch when another explosion shook the ground before a plane shot past overhead in what felt like only a few yards off the ground. I hit the sand before the ditch hard and because I had my mouth open, gravel filled it. My forward momentum took me sliding into the ditch. I lay face down coughing and spluttering to clear my mouth but not daring to lift my head in case it got shot off. I felt sore on my arms and knees which I guessed must be grazed.

As I lay there the thought of being killed came into my head. This was real now and those blighters in the planes were trying to finish us off. Then right there in front of my eyes, half buried in the sand, was a small post card. I lifted my hand to get it and at that moment it was a most beautiful thing. The Mother Mary dressed in a blue robe kneeling at a wooden alter with an Eden scene behind her and an angel in pink in front.

The words on the bottom of the card said Annunciazione di Maria, Vargine. I has no idea what the words meant or how the card got into that ditch. I guessed later that an Italian soldier was in this same ditch at some stage and must have lost it. I decided then to keep that card with me in my pocket for the duration of the war.

The card George found when being attacked by Stuka's. Meaning – The announcement of the Virgin conception and the birth of Jesus by Archangel Gabriel. (George Frame collection)

When the guns stopped firing and the noise of the planes faded I popped my head over the side of the ditch to look towards the convoy. Smoke was billowing up from a burning truck. Chaps were running around, seemingly in all directions. Taffy called out if I was alright. He was in another ditch several yards away. We both got out of the ditches, dusting ourselves off. We looked around for Walter and when we couldn't see him we both worried about his wellbeing. Hurrying towards the convoy it was a relief to see he was all right and that our truck and anti-tank gun was intact.

I was shaken to see what the German bombs had done. Two trucks were on fire and an artillery gun looked wrecked. Some chaps were helping others, who were injured, to get to the truck that had the medical supplies. A fellow who had his arms around two others shoulders, dragging his feet along the ground, was bleeding from his head. Some other chap was moaning loudly and when I looked to see what it was about I saw his leg was badly mangled. I could see bone sticking out above his knee. Strangely his leg reminded me of mincemeat. No one was killed, but half a dozen chaps were to be sent back to the field hospital for treatment of their wounds.

Our Officer began shouting orders for us to pack up. The damaged trucks and gun were left and we set off quickly in case the planes came back.

We were all on edge after that, often looking skywards and imagining planes. There was one false alarm the next day that sent the convoy into chaos. This happened when a truck veered off the road followed by two others. I stopped the truck I was driving and we all debussed quickly thinking another plane attack was about to happen. Nothing did happen and the Officer was not pleased at all with our behaviour.

So that was my introduction to the real shooting World War II. Shot at by someone I did not see, then dive bombed by German Stuka planes. I had found a postcard in the ditch that I jumped into to get away from being bombed. Seeing some trucks destroyed and realising that chaps can get badly hurt. This situation was going to be far more dangerous than I had thought.

Did you know?

The Cruiser Mk VI, named Crusader, was the main British-built tank used in the Western Desert. It gained the reputation for being unreliable essentially due to break downs from engine failures from radiator fans wearing out and being very hard to replace and failures with the water pumps due to the sand. They were manufactured in Britain by Nufield.

The Crusader initially had 40mm of frontal armour and was armed with a 2 pounder gun plus an auxiliary machine gun turret. The Crusader II's frontal armour was increased to 49mm and the machine gun turret was removed. The Crusader III version of the tank was armed with the 6pdr gun.

Each variant was outgunned and out armoured by the German Panzer.

We had stopped at a well to top up the water supplies, checking first to see that the well had not been spiked by the retreating Germans. It had not. Then out of nowhere a large German bomber flew in low over us. It gave us one hell of a fright. We all scrambled to our trucks and made a dash away in case it came back. Not long after that we heard artillery and tanks firing reasonably close to the south east of our position. It didn't seem that far away. That seemed strange as we understood our chaps were in the south east regions and not the Germans or Italians. The CO had us stop and ready the guns. We were in a slight depression that prevented us being that obvious. Was this to be our first real action we wondered?

As I waited for something to happen I experienced a strange sensation. I was excited at the prospect we were about to fire the guns in anger at the enemy, the enemy we had signed up to defeat. Yet at the same time my mind raced towards Lorraine and how I wanted to stay alive to be with her again. Then a wave of fear came over me as the images of those poor souls we had seen and the carnage that had occurred brought back the reality of the situation. I could be killed in a few moments. Dealing with all these emotions nearly overwhelmed me.

Suddenly a column of trucks and tanks were sighted off in the distance. The CO identified them as Italian. They were not moving towards us, rather parallel heading in a northerly direction. We readied ourselves, loaded the gun and waited as the column disappeared behind a small hill. The CO thought they had not spotted us and gave the order that on his command we were to fire two rounds and then to get out of this place as fast as we could, using the low hill as cover. The enemy forces were much too large for us to fight off.

When the column emerged they obviously had not seen us because they continued along their route. When about a third of the column had become visible the CO ordered us to fire. All the anti-tank guns fired in unison. A supply truck blew up with a direct hit and the enemy column began to react. We did not fire our gun a second time. We re-attached it to the truck and made off in haste keeping the hill between us and the enemy so that the tanks in that column were not able to zero in on our position.

It was exhilarating at the time and my blood was pumping as we sped away. One of our guns had hit the truck and bang, it went up in smoke. Only later on did I wonder if anyone died.

Not long after that we saw a German bomber in the distance with smoke pouring out of one wing. We stopped to watch as it descended. Clearly the pilot was trying to get it back to his airfield, but he lost that battle when it disappeared behind some low hills. It may have been the plane that flew over us earlier on.

The CO decided we should go and investigate. It was deceptive how far away it was. We didn't get to it until early the next day because we had to traverse around a series of low hills and soft sand.

The pilot had managed to get the plane down without it blowing up, but it was badly damaged. The German crew were not with the plane. We searched around for a while but did not locate them. Some chaps searched the plane for any documents or anything else of use to our side.

Approaching the downed German bomber cautiously, no crew were found.

(George Frame collection)

After the inspection we travelled back to where we had come across the enemy column the day before where we found the truck we had blown up. Not far away were two gravel mounds, graves with the helmets of the dead soldiers on them. Some of the chaps were very happy about killing the enemy, Taffy saying 'That's two less to kill'. My emotions were mixed. I was glad it was not me in the grave. Thinking that the enemy would not hesitate to shoot me if they had the chance. It was good we had done our job. Sad someone back in Italy had lost sons though. Taffy said to me that evening as we talked about the blown up truck, "'Cheer up George. We have to kill those bastards before they kill us." He was right of course.

Inspecting damage done. (George Frame collection)

Taken off a destroyed Italian truck in Libya by George

(George Frame collection)

When some Hurricanes flew overhead and I wondered if they were from No.237 Squadron which was a Rhodesian fighter squadron operating in North Africa. (Interestingly at that time, the Squadron was commanded by an Eric Smith whose son, Russell, married my daughter Diann in Salisbury, Rhodesia in the 1960's.)

As we were making our way westwards to catch up with the main army group we passed a detachment of South African infantry readying themselves to attack an Italian stronghold closer to the coast to their north west. I wondered how many of them would make it to sunset. Not long afterwards we heard the machine gun fire that indicated they had started the assault.

We were aware that the push for Tobruk was on and soon there would be more action likely. When that push started the 7th Armoured Brigade made its advance north westwards but when German tanks were sighted to the east of them their advance was diverted. We had made good progress always keeping a close lookout for any dust clouds that could indicate other vehicles or tanks. After a quick stop to brew tea and to eat something, we received information that the Germans were attacking our chaps at Sidi Rezegh which by our reckoning was due north of our position. Our orders were to find a suitable place to repel any enemy advance along the track we were on if they tried to surround the chaps defending Sidi Rezegh.

Bedraggled and wary. (George Frame collection)

We drove back south eastwards along the track to find a spot that our CO felt we could defend and we began the strenuous task of digging in. The ground was rock hard so it was tough manual work. After a few hours we moved the anti-tank guns into place. Our gun stuck out like dogs balls as we had unfortunately selected a position that had solid rock a few feet under the sandy top soil. We then decided to collect random rocks to put around the front of the emplacement, so we spent another hour hauling rocks well into the evening. I said that one tank shell would obliterate the meagre rock wall, but was told the rocks were there to hide the gun which, after all that effort, they did not.

Learning that the Germans and Italians were north of us, and that it also seemed likely that the Germans were to our east and west, made us all tense. If the Germans were to our south then we were surrounded.

Once the manual effort of getting ourselves prepared was over and we had settled down to wait, the expectation that the Germans would come at any time made me feel sick in my stomach. A watch rotation was set up and I was lucky enough to avoid being on that. Because I had been driving all day and may be driving hell for leather back to Egypt tomorrow if the Germans broke through again, I was allowed to get an uninterrupted night's sleep. That was unlikely to happen because, while I was exhausted, I was too anxious. Unlike some of my pals who could just fall asleep at the drop of a hat, I struggled. I could not stop thinking about the images of those poor souls lying in the desert with holes in them. However whilst I dozed in and out of sleep, it seemed to me that I was awake the whole night.

Before dawn, when a sliver of light appeared on the horizon, the time when any attack would be likely, we were all up and ready. Hoping that we had not been seen digging in, otherwise we could expect artillery shells to come in at us, we waited. I sat on a pile of anti-tank shells stacked behind our gun waiting for something to kick off . But as the sun emerged behind us nothing did happen and we collectively breathed a sigh of relief.

Soon a column of our own tanks passed us. They were in an almighty hurry and all we did was wave at each other as they passed by. Later on several supply trucks passed us as these tanks always needed fuel.

The news which we received later that day was that the Germans and Italians had struck a blow against the chaps north of us and were making their way eastwards once again. It was incredulous. How was all this backwards and forwards possible? Orders were to move east back towards Gabr Saleh. We packed up our shells and stacked them on the truck, hooked up the anti-tank gun very quickly and were soon belting it back the way we had come. This certainly was a strange war!

When we saw a column of dust ahead of us, our collective hearts missed a beat. Was it a German or Italian armoured column? We stopped, binoculars were taken out and the approaching vehicles were scanned. Because of the confusion as to where the Germans and Italians were and that we understood the enemy had captured our vehicles and may be using them, we felt very apprehensive. We began to take up defensive positions which turned out to be shambolic as the approaching column of three vehicles were upon us very quickly. Having one's finger on the trigger of a gun, scared that those approaching may want to kill you, while waiting for an order to either fire or stand down is nerve racking. It is very easy to panic and pull the trigger. Fortunately we all kept our nerve. They turned out to be a "Jock" Column from the 7th Armoured Division on reconnoitre to harass any enemy in the vicinity. What a relief that was.

After they left us our CO gave us a brief outline of what seemed a bigger shambles than we had imagined was occurring. The New Zealand chaps near the Libyan border had taken the brunt of a lot of the fighting, but had held out against superior odds. Both sides had lost large numbers of trucks, tanks and guns as well as men. Elsewhere the Germans had overrun some of our positions capturing many lads.

We set off despondent, driving ever vigilant, expecting to bump into the enemy at any moment. The adrenalin was certainly pumping with increased nervous tension. In the late afternoon we stopped for a meal and tea break. We had been on the run with no meals since the previous evening. I had not eaten much last evening because my stomach was in a knot. Keeping a watchful eye, which reminded me of the Meerkats in Southern Africa, we hurriedly polished off the meal. We then set off to find a suitable overnight position. The concern remained that the Germans would catch us in a pincer movement.

We carried on for a few hours until, finding a spot not far from where the track did an 'S' bend, the CO said we were to dig in. Any armoured column coming along that track would have to navigate the 'S' bend. In this position our guns could attack them on their sides. This time our crew found a spot that allowed us to dig in behind a rocky mound. The ground was forgiving which I was thankful for seeing as I had to do a lot of the digging.

We had a day respite there. We occasionally heard the thunder of guns and saw several planes in the far distance.

Our anti-tank gun was in the depression we, or should I say I, had dug out. The lads had scavenged some spinifex bushes to scatter around and attach to netting in an attempt to camouflage ourselves. Off to our left were the two other guns which were also reasonably camouflaged.

The trucks were nearby ready to move if we had to get away in a hurry. We had put netting over them. I was not sure how effective that would be. Three humps in a row that distinctly looked like trucks. But with the heat of the day, from a distance, the mirage effect probably would make it look like small sand dunes.

Camouflage netting to hide the trucks and guns were not always that effective.

(George Frame collection)

It was bloody hot sitting in the blazing sun. We couldn't brew up any tea during the day. The smoke from a fire would be a give-away of our position to the Germans or Italians, if they were to pitch up.

We were under the netting doing nothing much in the mid-afternoon. Some of the lads were playing cards. I was lying down dozing when the alert went out that there was dust in the distance. Someone was making their way towards us along the track.

We rushed to our guns, crouching to avoid being spotted, moving about as best we could. Without the field glasses I could see the dust cloud and beneath it some vehicles. They were not moving at speed and therefore unlikely to be an armoured car column or supply trucks.

The word came out – tanks! I thought we could have done with the 25 pounder artillery right at that moment. At least then the Germans or Italians would be kept far away from us and would probably retreat. What this situation probably meant was an engagement at close range and I dreaded that prospect. We hoped the officer, peering through the binoculars, would see that the tanks were not Panzers. If they were we would be done for. It was an anxious time waiting for the verdict.

"Two or three tanks. Some infantry and one transport."

Someone asked what the tanks were. The question we all wanted answered.

"Italians" came the reply.

Welcome news as we now had a fighting chance. The element of surprise in these situations was essential. Knocking out the front tank was the key as that would block those behind. To knock out the tank before those on board could locate us was obvious.

The wait was nerve-racking. Horrible in fact. Someone was going to die shortly and I hoped to God it was not going to be me. We all fell silent, each in our own private thoughts. Our gun had been set to its full range and a trajectory which we hoped would hit the front tank with the first shot as it passed a rocky marker we had sighted just off to the right of the track and where one side of it had an incline and the other side was a sandy depression. We were to fire first. Depending on where our shell fell, the other chaps would then adjust their sights and range before shooting off their round. The three of us would go in that sequence until we hit the tank or they hit us.

The officer, constantly peered through his binoculars, passed information to us. The tension steadily mounted. Fortunately they did not see us. I suspected they were all weary in this heat.

"Fire!"

Our anti-tank gun shot off its shell with a thunderous bang and lurched backwards. Dust erupted all around us. A dead give-away to anyone looking to see where the shot came from.

I was busy re-loading the next shell so didn't see where our first shot landed. It did not hit the tank. I figured this given no one was celebrating. All I knew was that the next shell had to get into the gun barrel quickly.

Within seconds the second gun fired its shell. The third gun shot off a round. Having loaded the shell, I stepped back and immediately that round shot out of our gun. With dust everywhere, I picked up the next shell and loaded the gun. That was when I became aware by the reaction of the chaps that a tank had been hit. There was a delay as the chaps at the second gun readjusted their sighting before it fired. By the time the third gun fired we had re-sighted our own gun. There were still the other tanks.

An explosion erupted behind us. A tank had fired. Time was limited now before they found their range.

In the commotion of a moment like this, you sometimes get lost in doing what you have to do. I just kept re-loading and lost count.

"Cease fire!" shouted the officer.

The enemy was retreating, leaving behind the tank that had been hit. It was bellowing black smoke.

Elation overtook the fear of the short battle. We were alive!

Before the light disappeared some chaps went with the officer to check out the tank that had been hit. There was always the chance that enemy would be in ambush near or around the tank, so caution had to be exercised. The tank was hit with the armour piercing shell that killed the tank and its crew. Several soldiers had also been killed by our exploding shells. No injured were found so they must have taken those who were wounded with them.

The rumble of artillery before dawn woke us up. We broke camp before the light showed itself and as the dawn broke we came across another column of armoured cars. Once again we were unsure if these were the enemy in captured armoured cars but before we knew it they were upon us. They were South Africans who were looking for German supply trucks suspected to be five miles away in a south westerly direction. Any German supply trucks were targets because to disrupt Rommel's supply was an important tactic to disable his tanks. We learned from them that the South African soldiers were engaged in a battle with Germans at a place south west of our location near Bir el Gubi. That must have been the artillery fire we had heard in the early morning.

The Germans were not retreating. They had routed our chaps over several days where we had lost a lot of tanks and many of our soldiers had been killed. It was at this time Rommel was talked about amongst the chaps as being a brilliant tank commander and with his new tanks he seemed to be unstoppable.

The last thing you would want to stumble across, a German Panzer.

(George Frame collection)

At one point we received sad news that the Germans had overrun a British forward airfield and captured some Hurricane planes. The Germans would use the captured planes to ambush our troops and our orders were to shoot down any planes that came near us, even if it was a Hurricane. It was not always that easy to tell which was a Hurricane or a Spitfire and, on hazy days, whether a plane was ours or the Germans until it was really close.

We had stopped for the afternoon brew and everyone was edgy. The stop was going to be quick so we could get to wherever we were supposed to be going before dark. We had not heard any gun fire since that morning but were not entirely sure where the enemy were situated.

I had finished my tea and was making my way towards the cab of my truck when shouting caught my attention. My heart pounded because I thought the Germans were coming. I grabbed my rifle before moving to the back of the truck. Gunfire broke out from one of the trucks that had the AA gun. Then others started shooting.

I saw the plane coming in low. It was tipping its wings up and down which I thought was strange at the time but as others were shooting at it, I loaded my rifle and shot as well. Smoke started to come from the plane just as it flew overhead. The chaps continued firing up at it. Once it passed us the smoke increased before the plane crashed, sending a plume of black smoke up into the sky. A great cheer rose up that we had shot down a plane. Someone said it was a Hurricane and that he hoped the German pilot was killed. The plane was too close to the ground for the pilot to parachute out so he must have gone in with it.

The Officer ordered that a truck, loaded with several chaps, go to the crash site. After quite a while they came back and the lads were very sombre indeed. It was a Hurricane that we had shot down but it was not flown by a German. The pilot was one of ours. They said he had gunshot wounds and was found lying away from the burning plane. They had taken his dog tags and had buried him near his plane. We guessed the tipping of his wings was him trying to tell us he was one of ours and the fact he did not strafe us should have been a tell-tale sign. I had wondered at the time why the pilot had not shot at us as he approached. We were told later that he was a Canadian airman. I felt very sorry about that incident and often reflected on it because as he flew past I caught a glimpse of him. I had fired several rounds at the plane and wondered if I had shot him. I also wondered why he flew over us when there was the order to shoot down all planes. Was he not told? What must he have thought when we all started shooting wildly at him? He didn't even try to get away.

Early one morning we had heard the rumble of guns blasting away and planes began flying back and forth. Then suddenly it became a mad panic that quickly turned chaotic as it seemed that our whole army was withdrawing. Fortunately the Germans had not broken through where we were located so we were lucky not to have been caught up in the fighting. They had, however, got through with armour in some places and were routing our chaps whenever they could. When we got orders to fall back with haste we dashed towards Gabr Saleh. The chaps in the 7th and 4th Armoured Brigades were pulling back.

When the order came to move towards Sidi Omar as the Germans had tanks in that vicinity we were never quite sure if we were in Egypt or Libya. We came across a makeshift air strip and were overjoyed to find that the chaps there were ours. They gave us a wonderful reception, but they must have felt sorry for us as we looked bedraggled, dirty and unshaven, whereas they all looked tidy and well kept. We had a good meal and plenty of nice tea which I particularly enjoyed. I had many cups.

I took the opportunity to have a look at the four Hurricane planes, two of which were being worked on before they could fly out.

Our Officer told us that the Germans were reported to be crossing into Egypt south of Sidi Omar and this air strip was to be abandoned because of that advance. He had agreed with the boys in blue for us to move into a defensive position a few miles out towards the south west to stop any German armoured force reaching the air strip before they could evacuate it later that afternoon.

We left after thanking our hosts for the meal and tea, wishing them well. We moved to a low outcrop which we had passed on our way eastwards. It was a good vantage spot overlooking a vast flat area. We would be able to see the dust of any advancing tanks or other German or Italian vehicles for miles. We dug in as best we could, given the soil was as hard as nails, before unhooking the anti-tank guns and moving them into position. As always I parked my truck close by in case we had to beat a hasty retreat. In these cases a few moments delay could make all the difference. We put the camouflage netting up. But this was a risky business settling down in the mid-afternoon, because one could never be absolutely certain we had not been spotted by the Germans who could either attack us by plane or even zero their artillery in on us. It seemed that was the risk our Officer was prepared to take.

I wondered how this piddley little force of ours was going to stop a German armoured advance presumably with dozens of German Panzer tanks. As time passed we all hoped that the air force guys would hurry up and bugger off so we could get away as well.

We heard the Hurricanes take off as the afternoon waned and some explosions later which were set by those chaps, presumably destroying whatever had been left there. Before the evening came we packed up our position, attached the guns to the trucks and drove off eastwards into the semi-darkness to find a place to bed down for the night.

On our way eastwards towards Sidi Omar we passed Indian soldiers being trucked towards the front although it was jolly confusing where any front actually was. It seemed the Germans were all over the place.

Feeling very fortunate to be alive after the rush back to Egypt. George standing to the left.

(George Frame collection)

We then heard that Rommel was on the run. I wondered if anyone really knew what was actually happening. This was not how I had anticipated the war to be. I thought there would be a battle and that would be the end of it. Instead this looked very much like a yo-yo with everyone going back and forth.

Our anti-tank reserve group were ordered to press north onto Sidi Azeiz. Along the route from Fort Capuzzo to Sidi Azeiz we passed the evidence of burned out tanks and trucks from both sides, some still smouldering, with bodies lying in the sand. It must have been hell to have been involved in that battle which had occurred quite recently. It certainly brought a sense of relief not to have been involved, while at the same time remorse that we had been out of it while these poor buggers were being blown to pieces.

En-route to Fort Capuzzo. (George Frame collection)

It was late afternoon when we got to Sidi Azeiz. We had expected that we would stay there for a while, but we were told to head back south west towards Gabr Saleh where our chaps were battling Italians and in case Rommel tried to outflank the chaps fighting along the road from Sidi Azeiz to Sidi Rezegh, east of Tobruk.

German and Italian prisoners of war being guarded by Indian troops at Fort Capuzzo.

(George Frame collection)

We spent several days near Gabr Saleh moving back and forth so as not to be caught in one place by either German planes or any tanks or artillery that may be lurking in that part of nothingness. It was anxious times because we were in the dark as to what was happening.

A 'Desert Rat' Story

We heard that Cunningham had been replaced as overall commander of the Eighth Army by a chap called Ritchie who our CO didn't think much of. That inspired no confidence in us and at night the conversation was centred on speculating why Cunningham, who had seemingly beaten Rommel in the past month, had been replaced. We wondered whether he been promoted to a bigger job in the British invasion of France.

Operation Crusader

The extent of losses from this operation on both sides was large. While the British and Commonwealth forces suffered 17,700 casualties to 38,300 by the Germans and Italians, over 800 British tanks were destroyed or broke down against 340 Axis tanks. Whomever had the superiority in tanks and the ability to maintain their supply lines would win the war of attrition in North Africa. Both sides lost around 300 aircraft each.

George fooling around in an Italian great coat and helmet.

(George Frame collection)

Chapter Seven

The Germans and Italians were in retreat. Rommel had run out of tanks and those he had were short on fuel and ammunition. His supply lines were broken from bombing by the boys in blue. He was running for Tripoli with our chaps hot on his tail, trying to cut him off.

That was the news we received and it sounded excellent.

Rommel on the run was far better news than hearing he was on the attack. We thought, just maybe, this war in North Africa would soon come to an end.

We drove all day back along the track we had been on days before. When we got close to El Adam we came across the aftermath of a battle. It must have been hell on earth to be in the middle of it.

Abandoned and burned out Afrika Korps equipment. (George Frame Collection)

The aftermath of the battles left scrap metal scattered all over the desert.

(George Frame collection)

We felt quite numb when we passed the burned out tanks and other vehicles scattered over the desert. I secretly thanked heavens that we had once again avoided this. I wondered if, after the war, there would be a business opportunity to collect all the scrap metal.

Tobruk had been relieved. The chaps, sieged in Tobruk, mostly Australians, had strongly defended themselves from the Rommel's Afrika Korps under very harsh conditions. New Zealanders had been in the thick of the battles around the Tobruk area and had lost a lot of soldiers.

The lifting of the siege was a cause to celebrate which we did by having a brew of tea!

We stayed close to El Adam, south of Tobruk, for a while taking the time to clean and check that our weapons were in working order. With the sand it was always a worry the equipment would get clogged up. We also restocked on munitions, water and food when the supply trucks arrived. During our time there columns of tanks and supply vehicles moved west towards Acroma. The Front was dynamic and had quickly moved west of Tobruk towards Gazala on the coast.

We were informed that we were to be attached to a reserve section called Mayfield for the next stage of whatever the Generals had in mind. I thought that name certainly did not reflect the reality of what was around us. Desert. Heat. Dust. Death and destruction. One wondered where they came up with such ridiculous names.

Camp south of Tobruk. Rows of graves in the background.

(George Frame collection)

When we received the order to move out it was not to the Front along the coast, but to the south west. Our destination was Bir Hacheim. On the map it was a dot in the middle of nowhere and we wondered why there. I heard that there was a fort of some kind and an oasis which I thought could be interesting to see.

We joined in a convoy of armoured cars and tanks loaded on transports. During the following day the main part of the column turned west while we carried southwards to Bir Hacheim. Our objective was to once again track south of the main force in case Rommel tried to outflank the advance. We understood that our chaps were trying to get across the desert to the south of Bengazi to cut the enemy retreat off and that many enemy had surrendered during the advance when they had been overrun. Given the options available I wondered if they were not just being smart to be captured.

Bir Hacheim was a total disappointment. But it was an oasis, in a very non-romantic sense of the word, in a sea of sand. Nonetheless we were grateful for the brief respite after we set up a camp. That afternoon I wrote letters to my darling Lorraine and my parents. We spent our days checking and rechecking the weapons and anti-tank guns, servicing the trucks and making sure spare tires were in good order. I did manage to see the well that the Romans had dug there so very long ago.

Time to relax in the middle of nowhere. (George Frame collection)

At one stage during our time at Bir Hacheim chaps in armoured cars pitched up. They spent a day and night with us. They were from the Hussars and were a pretty bedraggled bunch having been scouring the vastness of the desert for weeks in search of the enemy. They told us of some of the action they had been involved with which was impressive. Mainly harassing German and Italian supply lines, attacking supply columns, but avoiding direct action with German tanks. They left us more refreshed and cleaner than when they arrived.

Some chaps we came across at Bir Hacheim. (George Frame collection)

We received the news that our chaps had been delayed in cutting off the enemy retreat at Bengazi due to bad weather. It had rained which turned the roads and desert tracks into mud that bogged the tanks and other vehicles.

While Bir Hacheim was in no way paradise, I had hoped to spend Christmas there rather than somewhere in the middle of who knows where, not that Christmas would mean anything really given what we were experiencing. But a week before Christmas we received orders to move out and head westwards in support of our chaps who were moving towards a place called Msus.

Did you know?

The term "Desert Rats" was ascribed to the 7[Th] Armoured Division because of its emblem which was a red Jerboa, a nocturnal rodent indigenous of North Africa. Meanwhile the 7th Armoured Brigade adopted a green Jerboa as its emblem and once this Brigade moved to Burma in 1942 it became known as the 'Jungle Rats'.

Because we understood that the Germans and Italians were unlikely to be in the vicinity we drove quite fast. Our meal and tea breaks were short and we travelled until it was dark, then we were up and moving again at first light. I rotated driving the truck with Taffy because driving all day was really tiring on the sandy tracks. We did not stop to have a look when we passed several destroyed tanks, guns and trucks, both ours and German and Italian.

The CO told us that Msus was clear of the enemy and that the Germans had left Benghazi. It was reported that the Germans used the Italian navy to evacuate Benghazi so as not to be caught in the encirclement trap. I was surprised to get that news as I thought that the Italian Navy would have been blown up by the Royal Navy and the Med was controlled by the British. Clearly not.

The push was on for Beda Fomm and consequently our orders changed to move northwards towards Benina, east of Benghazi. We had travelled through Christmas day. It came and passed without celebration. There was nothing to celebrate in any event as 'peace on earth and goodwill to all mankind' was farcical. Seeing burned out tanks and trucks and smelling the stench of decaying mutilated bodies was not conducive to that message. Both sides were more than likely to be praying to God to win this bloody conflict so it would end.

The endless expanse of nothingness on a flat lifeless landscape.

(George Frame collection)

When we got near Benina we discovered many of our tanks and trucks were stationary along the track. They were intact and they had their crews with them, but they had run out of fuel! The fuel supply trucks had not arrived having been left behind as the push towards Benghazi was so fast. We were short of fuel and water ourselves so were unable to share, but it did make us think that it was now an awfully long way to Cairo or Alexandria where the fuel had to come from.

We pressed on to Benina to find it had an airfield. When we approached the air field we saw German planes there and we immediately halted, worried that the Germans had not left. We saw people milling around at the airfield, but only after the CO looked through his field glasses did we know they were our chaps. Why did the Germans leave so many planes behind I asked myself? The answer soon became obvious. The rains had made the airfield muddy and the planes were bogged in. I wondered why the Germans had not blown up the planes if they could not fly them out. Even their tents were still there. Perhaps our advance had been so quick that they were caught by surprise.

The Germans left Benina in a hurry! (George Frame Collection)

I was fascinated when I was able to get up close to the planes, especially the Stuka. The engine cowling was off the Stuka exposing its engine. I was impressed at the size of its engine and wondered if this was the bloody plane that had dropped its bombs on us months before.

German 109 left behind a retreating army.

(George Frame collection)

The Stuka's were superb aircraft. Left abandoned in the rush of retreat.

(George Frame collection)

We set up camp at Benina not knowing how long we would stay there but looking forward to a period of rest after many days of solid driving. But rest was not on the agenda. The CO wanted all the vehicles checked and the anti-tank guns and our own weapons cleaned. He tasked Taffy and me to go and scavenge fuel because our trucks were all on empty. The jerry cans were also empty.

Taffy and I set off on the search, but after a short while we realised it was a fruitless task. To find fuel, given what we had seen on the way into Benina, with many vehicles and tanks having run out of fuel, was going to be a miracle. No one was going to give us any fuel that was certain. But we did not want to go back too soon otherwise we would have to get involved in the cleaning and servicing. We were tired, so we found a spot shaded by a building and settled down. I fell asleep. The CO was not pleased when we returned hours later empty handed, but he bought our story that we had searched high and low. We at least avoided the chores which were done by the time we got back. The following morning we managed to get fuel when the supply trucks arrived.

We then got permission to go into Benghazi for a day. It was far bigger than I had imagined. There was extensive damage to many buildings and roads with holes all over the place from the bombing. The locals seemed happy to see us and cheered the troops as they drove through the city. I guessed they had done the same to the Italians when they came and also to the Germans. I suspected they were not that attached to any of us. The Union Jack flew from several buildings. Interesting how the flag demonstrated ownership no matter how transient it may be. A day or so before the Nazi flag would have been flying proudly.

I wanted to do two things. To see the Mediterranean and to have a beer so Taffy, Walter and I set off towards the coast. Along the way we were harassed by young local lads wanting anything they could get hold of. We had nothing to give and it became annoying. Walter chased them away at one stage and they gave some verbal abuse back at us before running off to find others to pester.

It was glorious to see the blue water after the long months stuck in the desert. I ran down to the sea edge, took off my boots and socks, rolled up the trousers and waded in. We all splashed about like children for quite some time, getting drenched. Why we didn't strip off and dive in I don't know.

From the beach side, looking towards the city, you could see that this place had been a bustling port and prosperous commercial centre. Smoke either from burning buildings, tanks or trucks was still rising from many parts. The harbour had some sunken ships in it.

On our way back we managed to find a vendor who sold us three beers and some type of bread. Everything was a haggle, but Walter eventually settled it by shouting at the vendor suggesting he would be shot. The beers were warm but we didn't mind that. After such a long dry spell, the alcohol went to our heads.

Our stay at Benina was short lived. More re-supply trucks arrived and we got the fuel we required and stocked up on food supplies, even tea, which I was very pleased about. A few weeks before the tea had tasted foul. It was actually disgusting. I discovered that the chap who had brewed it was straining the tea leaves through his vest which was caked with his sweat!

Convoys of equipment and armour moved through towards Ajedabia which was where Rommel had drawn a line in the sand. We then heard that our chaps had been given a beating south of Ajedabia. Many of our tanks and artillery were lost as Rommel had attempted to outflank the Eighth Army. We felt very fortunate that we had been diverted to Benina because had we not been we probably would have been caught up in that battle given Rommel had broken through the lines.

We received our orders to quickly move to the Ajedabia line where we could expect to see some action. We would be travelling along the coastal road through Beda Fomm, then going inland in a southerly direction from the coastal region. Given Rommel had often outflanked our chaps, it didn't look encouraging that he would not try the same again and this time we would be there.

When we came across destroyed and abandoned Italian military equipment I was told these were from the battles a year before. It was fascinating to look at these burned out carcasses of vehicles which told the story of violence. Mounds of sand in uneven rows told the story of death.

Italian artillery was abandoned during the battle of Beda Fomm

(George Frame collection)

The Italian artillery was abandoned during the battle of Beda Fomm

(George Frame collection)

Close by we came across the bodies of unburied soldiers forcing me to gag. Our Officer told us to make sure we were not like that corpse and to keep our wits about us.

Not all the casualties of war were buried. The remnants of the battle.

(George Frame collection)

The story was that the Italians had been on the run, hell for leather for Tripoli, but had lost most of their army in February 1941 in a battle near Beda Fomm as part of Operation Compass. This was before we arrived in North Africa.

As I understood it, the Italians were totally demoralised, were a spent force, and all they wanted to do was get home to Italy. But then the Germans had arrived in numbers, catching the British napping with extended supply lines. The Germans apparently had better tanks and, with Rommel as their General, they were altogether a different kettle of fish from the Italians. Pushed back across Libya by the Germans, our chaps had taken a beating. The Aussies were trapped at Tobruk. An earlier attempt to relieve Tobruk had failed. The main plan of this current offensive was to relieve them which had been successful.

Derailed train near Benghazi (George Frame Collection)

Did you know?

The battle at Beda Fomm in February 1941 was a resounding victory for the British against a numerical superior Italian and Libyan army. The consequence of which was to force Hitler to send more German troops to North Africa to stop the defeat of Italian forces there.

For the loss of 500 dead, 1,373 wounded and 55 men missing the British had advanced 500 miles and destroyed the back bone of the Italian army when the 10th Army surrendered. During Operation Compass of which the battle at Beda Fomm was its culmination, the British took over 133,000 prisoners, including twenty two generals, the Italian general staff and over 960 guns and armour of all types was captured or destroyed.

We soon came to a where there had been an almighty tank battle the day before. The scene there was just terrible. There were tanks, trucks and guns destroyed scattered all over. The Germans had won the battle insofar as they knocked out more tanks than they sustained losses but for some reason had withdrawn from the fight.

Inspecting the damage done to German's equipment. (George Frame collection)

We spent the next day burying dead soldiers. Soldiers caught in tanks when hit with armour piercing shells are terribly mutilated, many burned so badly they don't resemble human corpses. It is truly horrible.

I volunteered to dig graves rather than recover bodies so as to avoid, as much as possible, the stench of burned flesh which was overpowering. Some of those poor chaps having to retrieve bodies vomited until their diaphragms ached. I hated staring into the glassy eyes of the bodies laid out ready to be put into the holes.

The German dead were treated equally to our own. I actually found myself feeling as sorry for them as I did for our own chaps.

Tank crew suffered horrible injuries.

(George Frame collection)

There had been many wounded soldiers from this battle, some with terrible burns, being treated in a field hospital before being transported back. Several died in the field hospital and they had to be fetched to be buried.

I do not know how many we buried other than I dug an awful lot of graves and I was one among so many others doing that task.

My appetite was curtailed. I struggled for a long time afterwards to get restful sleep. Every time I closed my eyes I could see those poor broken bodies, glassy eyes and smell the burned flesh. It was around this time that my faith in religion evaporated. I had never really been that religious, certainly not a regular church goer other than when forced to in school in Britain. There it was compulsory to attend church every Sunday. I had been educated in Christianity, said prayers and had believed in God. That belief in a God just went. I could not believe that any God overlooking this Earth could allow such carnage. We had prayed for God's guidance in winning this war. The Italians did that also. And I was damned sure the Germans did so too. Yet this wanton killing was taking place each day here in the desert, in Europe and in the Far East. This was when my belief in a God flew away.

Displaying the German flag found as spoils of war. (George Frame collection)

We spent a few days south of Ajedabia expecting something to happen. Our nerves were on edge given what we had recently witnessed and the lack of real knowledge of what was going on did not help relieve the tension. Rommel had moved his army back along the coast to El Agheila and there was a lull in the fighting. This always preceded a battle. The lull was when both sides took stock, re-equipped and prepared themselves for the next round.

We heard that the South Africans had beaten the enemy at Sollum taking many prisoners. That was good news to get, although I was unaware that there was still enemy forces so far east and wondered how they had managed to hold out for so long.

We spent time doing very little other than driving here, there and then back again in an expanse of nothingness. The days drifted into one another as the routine was the same. Rise before sunrise, pack up and move off, stop after the sun had come up for breakfast and a brew, before heading off to wherever the Officer decided we should stop. When we stopped for the long break we would set up a tarpaulin for shade and rest. Someone would keep watch with binoculars. That task was rotated amongst us and it was not a simple task. The mirages thrown up by the heat were deceptive and the chaps did not take it lightly when a false alarm was raised. Scrambling around only to find it was nothing always resulted in some repercussion for the poor sod who made the false call. It was also quite a task to stay alert when on the lookout duty. I often found my head wobbling around as sleep challenged my concentration. I actually fell asleep on occasion.

Meal time. (George Frame collection)

The monotony made some chaps get edgy. Squabbles became more frequent and the occasional rough and tumble occurred. I for one was quite content not to be risking the opportunity to get shot at, and besides, I was generally comfortable with my own company. Taffy and Walter were good company and we tended to stick together still regarding ourselves as the '3 musketeers'. Taffy had a scuffle with a chap over food portions and was grabbed by the neck. His feet were hardly touching the ground and his face turned a crimson colour through his dark tan. Walter saw the incident and called me. The two of us rushed up and we 'persuaded' the other chap to let Taffy down gently. He kept out of our way after that.

Two of the 3 Musketeers. (George Frame collection)

When we learned that the United States had declared war against Hitler's Germany we leapt for joy. Running around like mad things relieved some of the pent up tension. In our minds that meant the war would soon come to an end. How could the German Army win when fighting the Americans at the same time as Britain and the Russians? I did not understand why the Japs had bombed Pearl Harbour, but was grateful that they did as now the Americans had come in. Their industrial power was bound to bring this war to a speedy end.

The lull in action was not to last. Expecting an attack south of the coast where we were located, Rommel attacked along the coastal area. At the time we were near El Haseia. Our CO said our orders were to hold our position and watch out for any German advance in an attempt by them to encircle our chaps at Ajedabia. But the next day we heard the Germans had pushed through Ajedabia and were making for Msus with their tanks. This meant that all of us in the area south of Ajedabia could be cut off if Rommel's forces pushed through Msus and advanced to Benghazi or towards Bir Hacheim. It seemed to me at that time to be obvious that we should get back, but there appeared to be some confusion with the information our CO was getting. The confusion cleared up quickly the following day when we got news that the Germans had got to Msus and had beaten our chaps there in a quick engagement.

The terrain was unrelenting – sand and rocks as far as one could see.

(George Frame collection)

We therefore had to get back before we got trapped behind the enemy lines so we set off in haste towards Tengeder. It was a long, arduous trek through nothingness along rough tracks, full of rocks and gullies. We drove all day and into the night with short stops. Our radiators overheated at times and tyres blew which caused anxious delays. My truck was okay although at times steam came from the bonnet. My arms ached and my neck muscles tightened, giving me a headache from driving. Along the way we heard, from chaps in an armoured car convoy we came across, that the Germans were advancing on Mechilli and Benghazi. One had to wonder how the heck the Germans had achieved this rapid advance.

The Germans captured many of our tanks intact and we were told that they would use them against us, seeing their own tank numbers were down. Matilda tanks were identified as those we had to watch for in case they were manned by Germans. This made a confused situation even more complicated for me because, as an anti-tank gunner, I was not about to wait until the tanks were running us over before we figured out if they were manned by our chaps or the enemy, and it was unlikely any Germans driving our captured tanks would tell us in advance.

Rommel, the Desert Fox. Picture developed from a camera picked up by George in the desert.

(George Frame collection)

Did you know?

Erwin Rommel was born in Heidenheim, Germany, on November 15, 1891. He was the son of a teacher. Rommel joined the German infantry in 1910 and fought with the rank as a lieutenant in World War I in battles in France, Romania and Italy.

Rommel was named commander of the 7th Panzer division in 1940 and in the following year he was appointed commander of German troops (the Afrika Korps) in North Africa.

Italian losses to the British in North Africa caused Hitler to send Rommel to Libya, where he reversed the losses and laid siege to the port city of Tobruk from April to December 1941. His forces were repulsed by the British but he regrouped and he returned with the Afrika Korps in June 1942 to take the city. This attack became known as the Battle of Gazala. He was then promoted to Field Marshal by Adolf Hitler.

Rommel's military talent was undoubtedly his strategic conceptual ability of the battle and for his decisive personal leadership. He had a capability above all for the speed and energy with which he decided and acted.

Rommel's most significant achievement in the war was his defeat of the British at Gazala in May 1942, followed by the taking of Tobruk.

At El Alamein however he lost the initiative and then the North African campaign as the Eighth Army under Bernard Montgomery won convincing victories as Rommel was forced to withdraw the survivors of his *Panzerarmee* to Tunisia. The Americans had landed in North Africa and were moving east, the British Eighth Army had reconquered Tripolitania and was on the Tunisian border which hemmed the Germans in. Being isolated and facing overwhelming odds Rommel left for Europe in March 1943.

Despite his defeat in North Africa, Rommel carried his reputation for leading his army from the front rather than the rear. His nickname the "Desert Fox" for his surprise attacks stuck with him and while in North Africa he also gained popularity in the Arab world as a liberator from British rule. At home in Germany he became known as the "the People's Marshal," and was heralded as both one of Hitler's most successful generals and one of Germany's most popular military leaders.

Rommel was entrusted with the Channel coast's defence against a possible Allied invasion in early 1944. At that time having seen what was happening to his home land with the aerial bombing and the tragedy on the Russian Front, Rommel doubted Hitler's capability to lead the nation. He was associated with conspirators who planned the unsuccessful plot to overthrow Hitler. Hitler decided to offer Rommel the option of taking his own life to avoid a public trial and to protect his family, a consideration not given to other conspirators.

On the October 14, 1944, several German officers took Rommel to a remote location. Biting into a cyanide capsule he took his own life. He was 52 years old and was given a full military burial.

It was becoming quite obvious that this desert war would be won by those who had the supply lines in tact to resupply the soldiers and in particular the fuel for trucks and tanks. Bringing the supplies from Alexandria to Benghazi was as long a trek for us as it was for Rommel to bring his supplies from Tripoli eastwards. I wondered why the boys in blue were not able to bomb Rommel's supply lines and why the Royal Navy could not stop the enemy's ships getting across the Med which would cripple his ability to fight us.

We had our own problem to contend with being the lack of fuel and water, both of which had to be carefully used. We were however lucky to hook up with a supply column and managed to get our jerry cans refilled with fuel, resupplied the water and we also scrounged some tins of food. Prior to that lucky occurrence, we had wondered how we were actually were going to make it to Bir Hacheim.

Supply was a critical aspect of the battle and who would eventually win the war.

(George Frame collection)

By the time we got to Bir Hacheim we were exhausted. It was fortunate that along the way we did not encounter the Germans or Italians. We did however come across some locals but they were largely unfriendly, tending to avoid contact with us. I wondered what they thought what was going on. Presumably they thought we were all crazy driving back and forth, shooting and killing each other in the middle of nowhere. I had the same thoughts at this stage.

We stopped for a day at Bir Hacheim but were fully occupied in once again cleaning the guns, servicing the trucks and restocking on whatever we could scavenge. The CO obsession with cleaning the weapons and servicing the trucks, while painful, was actually one of the most sensible actions to take. The news that Benghazi had fallen was a shock to us, but then to hear that the Germans were advancing towards Derma was very disturbing. To think of all the lives lost in the battles to push the Germans back had been for nothing. That Rommel's army was making such fast progress demoralised us all.

The Free French Foreign Legion were building defences at Bir Hacheim while the remnants of the Indian soldiers who had been stationed there were preparing to re-join their divisions further north. Some sort of box defensive strategy was engaged from the coast to Bir Hacheim to stop Rommel advancing east with the expectation was this would stop his army.

The French were a sultry lot. I suppose the fact that we could not speak French was not of any help.

Our orders were to move north towards Gazala where our chaps were digging in to halt Rommel. Benghazi was lost. The CO told us we would probably see action and that we should write letters home before we set off. I wondered where we would post them, but I did take the time to write to Lorraine and my parents. I hoped not to convey the disillusionment I felt at this confused, and what seemed a pointless, war in the desert.

As we made our way northwards we became more anxious about what was going to happen. A gloom fell upon us all because we felt defeated. Clearly the Germans were not beaten as we thought. The likelihood of facing the Germans was more real now than ever. We assumed that their tank commanders were war hardened and thus quick to react, whereas for us, we had not fired a shot in anger for a long time. All we had done was to drive back and forth across expanses of desert, clean our guns at every occasion and wait. The big question we all had on our minds, but did not dare say it, was whether we were up to it and of equal fighting preparedness to the enemy. We had been informed that the 2-Pounder anti-tank guns that we had were proving ineffective against the newer German armour in the battles and I worried how long we would survive having to fire the gun at virtually point blank range. To hit a tank where the turret joined the main body of the tank was a one in a hundred chance strike. Hitting the Panzer where its armour was thickest was like throwing a stone at it.

When we arrived at Alem Hamda we received orders to travel east to a place that had been set up to re-supply the troops and that we could get new equipment. At first we thought it would be new trucks from America. Ours were pretty beaten up, although the engine of mine was working well. When we arrived we were delighted to find that we were getting new anti-tank guns. Brand spanking new 6-Pounders!

6-Pounder anti-tank gun and its transport truck. (George Frame collection)

There were a few of the 2-Pounder anti-tank guns mounted on trucks. We were buoyed by the new arrivals and the news that more tanks were arriving daily for the Eighth Army. These tanks were called Grant and they had two cannons. They looked far superior to what our chaps had been using. With these armaments we surely would push Rommel back to Tunisia in no time. At least that was what we told each other to lift the gloom.

The training on use of the new guns took two days which I did not mind at all. The meals at the depot were far better than those we had been having. There was plenty of water and even some beers were scrounged. It was good to be able to talk to some other chaps and we associated best with the South Africans, given we were from the same part of Africa. They had seen a lot of action. Their stories of the recent fighting were horrible. Some of the chaps seemed a bit crazy and I guessed that is what happened when being exposed to such things. I hoped that when our time came I would not go that way.

The only problem I had was that the shells for the 6- Pounder were far heavier and having to load them into the barrel tired me out quicker. My back, neck and arms ached more than usual. The gun blasted out a louder noise and so after a few shots my ears hummed. Once loaded, I had to grab another shell so was not able to cover my ears when the blast went off. The recoil also was far more severe. Some chaps were hurt from the recoil. Its range was better which I was happy about as this meant we could keep the distance between us and the enemy tanks that much farther away.

Each anti-tank gun section now had six men, two of them armed with Tommy Guns. The rest of us still had .303's. The metal shield on the gun was thicker and larger than what we had before but it was really inadequate to protect all of us from gun fire and in particular any shell from a Panzer tank. We knew that we had to be accurate within the first few shots before a tank would zero in on us and blow us to hell.

Our own defence – two chaps with machine guns to shoot advancing infantry.

(George Frame collection)

The tyres on the 6-Pounders were exposed so any shot hitting them would render the gun essentially immobile. A good thing was the ease in which we were able to unhitch the gun and set it in position. We did this over and over until we managed it like a well-oiled wheel. By the time we had finished the training we felt more confident that we would be able to acquit ourselves if we had to.

Did you know?

Rommel used tactics that outwitted the old cavalry ethos used by the British tank commanders. This outdated approach of transposing tanks with how the British had used horses in cavalry charges had cost the British dearly, yet they continued to use that approach. The Auk's formations as they had become known failed to master the Afrika Korps' tactic of letting the British armour fall against the anti-tank guns before they themselves committed their Panzers.

We moved to a position south of Gazala. Still operating as a reserve mobile unit our objective was to stop any enemy tanks that breached the line west of us. There was a large land mine field laid down between us and the enemy forces, plus a box line defence system. Any enemy tanks would need to get through those obstacles first then get past our tanks, anti-tank guns and artillery before we would have to challenge them. We felt reassured that the enemy would be unable to achieve that.

There was a long period where nothing happened. It was a weird sensation because we knew this period was the calm before the next battle but not knowing if this calm would last a week, a month or longer yet knowing it would surely end, was unnerving.

In the meantime each side prepared for it. We cleaned the guns regularly as the wind always blew sand everywhere. I lost track of time and the date other than the nights were still very cold.

When the action came it took us by surprise. I had been under the impression, as were the others in our group, that we were preparing to make a big push against the Afrika Korps. But rather than us attacking the enemy positions, the Italians and Germans attacked first and against Bir Hakeim which I gathered was not expected. It had started with an almighty artillery barrage followed by their tanks advancing.

It was late May.

The order to mobilise came with the information that Rommel had transited south of Bir Hakeim. News on what had occurred was sketchy other than it was suspected that German tanks were to our south which was behind our defensive line. We scrambled into our trucks and waited for news. Expectant that their aircraft would attack we kept a watchful eye on the western skies. I wondered when our boys in blue would fly over us and shoot the Germans and Italians to bits.

We eventually transited south and dug the anti-tank guns in preparing ourselves for an expected attack. Violent tank fire erupted alerting us to a tank battle close to us. The dust was bad with a strong wind blowing sand into us. The reduced visibility made me feel really worried. We would have little time to zero in on a tank coming at full speed towards us when it emerged out of the dust haze. We were yet to fire the new anti-tank guns in anger so there was a lingering doubt if, when push came to shove, we would perform well enough to stay alive.

It all happened in a flash and a blur. Tanks emerged through the haze ahead of us with soldiers following behind. Before I could really grasp the situation the anti-tank guns on our right fired a salvo, then our gun fired.

The chaps yelled at me to load another shell into the barrel. I bent down to pick up a shell when an almighty explosion sent rocks and sand all over us. I could hear the zip, zip of bullets all around. As I picked up the shell the chap next to me, Thomas, who was our machine gunner, threw his arms up and let the gun drop. He fell only feet away from me face down. His uniform was covered in blood. The sound of the bullet hitting him was something I had never heard the like of before.

"Load the bloody shell!" shouted Walter.

That snapped me out of being transfixed with Thomas's blood seeping into the sand around him. Our other machine gunner was firing at the enemy and other anti-tank guns were blasting away. The atmosphere was filled with smoke and dust. Hearing the Panzer shells wiz overhead with a woosh, woosh sound was frightening. When our tanks engaged the enemy we found ourselves in the middle of it all. The whole situation was terribly confusing and frightening.

Our gun was hit and it lurched back knocking Walter, who was target aiming, and Taffy who was working the trajectory mechanism, to the ground. I thought they had been hit and killed. My emotions spun in turmoil. I was scared that the Germans would overrun us and we would get stabbed with bayonets. Being shot and killed outright was better than being stabbed in the belly by a bayonet. Seeing my dear pals lying on the ground having witnessed poor Thomas being shot dead suddenly made me so angry.

I was so relieved when both Walter and Taffy got up. They were shaken but seemed okay. We looked to see if the gun was still able to be used. It was, except for a large dent on its front armour shield and one tyre was shredded. We worked fast to get the gun back to its original position, then, adjusting its trajectory, we were operational once again.

Amongst abject confusion the enemy's advance seemed to stall and they withdrew. A tank quite close to us was on fire and suddenly the shells inside exploded, blowing its turret off. It made a tremendous bang. An anti-tank gun, 50 yards to our right, was destroyed and chaps were assisting the wounded, some of whom were screaming from their injuries. We learned later that legs and arms had been blown off a few of them when a tank shell scored a direct hit.

German tank knocked out by George's crew. (George Frame collection)

Afterwards we sat in stunned silence huddled behind our gun looking at Thomas who lay there on the ground covered in sand and small rocks. The blood stain was not visible. It was a horrible sensation. Each of us was very sad that a fellow soldier had been killed, yet thankful it was not us. We fetched a blanket from the truck to cover Thomas's body. The truck had been hit many times with bullets and I hoped the engine had not been damaged given we may yet have to make a speedy exit from here. Later on when I got into the cab the engine started much to my relief. The front seat was worse for wear as a bullet entering the side door had torn it up.

Thomas was taken away. We retrieved the blanket. Walter had a medic look at his arm which was bleeding badly. Luckily or unluckily, depending upon the individual's perspective, it was not broken. If it was he would be sent back, away from this terrible place. I had sand in my eyes that caused me a lot of irritation so I had to rinse them with water from a water bottle.

My mind was numb and I did what needed to be done without really thinking much.

Our reprieve was short lived. The order was to get the 'hell out of here' and we frantically extracted the gun from its dug in position and replaced the wheel. Fortunately the axil was not damaged so it was able to be attached to the truck and pulled. We then loaded up the trucks and moved north.

We had believed that the mine field between us and the enemy was obviously a factor why the Italians or Germans would not be able to attack us in force. It was not always easy to traverse through a mine field. As it turned out the sly Desert Fox had come around and not through the mine fields.

A land mine. (George Frame collection)

The next few days were very tense not knowing exactly where the Germans were and what we were supposed to be doing. We became emotionally and physically exhausted with our adrenalin constantly running high. We were very twitchy, startled at any noise. We expected the German tanks to emerge at any moment. We half expected the Stukas would bomb us, but that didn't happen either. They did bomb our chaps in other spots along the defensive corridor though. We were just lucky, I guess, to be missed.

One night a chap on guard started firing his machine gun which got us all up in a hurry and firing wildly into the darkness. Poor fellow was taken away to a field hospital with his nerves shot to pieces. The tension, bombardments and fighting must have got the better of him. I was tired, anxious and jumpy so could see how that was possible. Seeing our tanks gave us some respite to our anxiety believing they offered us a fighting chance.

Always good to have our tanks close at hand

(George Frame collection)

The RAF flew over a few times but because we were so on edge, we would always scramble for cover. I wondered what the RAF pilots thought seeing us scattering about. We would all be sitting around with hardly anyone talking when someone would cock his head. Immediately others would do the same straining to catch the sound of what that fellow had heard. Then something would set us off and in unison we would all rush off like scalded cats to our guns or find cover. Afterwards we would all have a nervous laugh. There was nothing really funny. It was nerves and the laugh allowed us to relieve the tension, even if only for a moment.

Whenever we stopped our chaps would be looking out for the German air force.

(George Frame collection)

When the alarming news came that Rommel was at Sidi Mufta, which was close to our position, we were ordered to hold our position. Some of the South Africans were being sent to join the Indian division to ward off this move by the Germans. The tanks that had been with us moved towards the enemy position leaving us feeling very vulnerable.

We often saw smoke rising either from battles or attacks on supply columns. We were attacked with shell fire soon after taking this picture. (George Frame collection)

We learned that there was heavy fighting going on in what was to be called The Cauldron in an effort to stop Rommel pushing a corridor through the mine fields and, in so doing, enabling him to get reinforcements then to encircle and defeat us.

A sand storm just added to the discomfort with everything getting covered in sand, our equipment, blankets, clothes, food; the lot. At least the dust storm would have grounded the German Stukas. But then it also grounded our planes, so which was better?

We were having our evening meal when the order came to evacuate fast because we may all now be encircled and likely to be captured. We worked frantically to get the 6-Pounders hooked up to the trucks. While we were preparing to leave the CO was trying to ascertain what was happening, but the radio communications were not operating that well.

For some reason in the confusion that followed, I ended up behind the wheel of our supply truck with Walter. Taffy was in the passenger's seat of the truck pulling the 6-Pounder. Once we started moving it became very hard to see anything in the dark because the dust blurred the vision of the dim headlights. I had no idea where we were supposed to be going other than Tobruk had been mentioned and that we were supposed to link up with the South Africans to our north. It became chaotic with all the vehicles and soldiers moving at the same time in the dark.

After a while we heard the sound of shelling ahead of us. When we stopped the CO directed us to change direction. I think he thought we were heading straight into the enemy. After many hours driving we ended up quite far south. I thought we were lost. In the dim light of the dawn we did manage to link up with other trucks and some armoured cars all making a dash southwards. I hoped the officers knew what they were doing as I certainly had no idea of where we were heading.

By the early morning we were south of Bir Hacheim which we later gathered was in German hands. I asked myself if we were going to the Sahara Desert to join the French Foreign Legion. However we turned east in a mad dash towards Bir el Gubi. It was a frantic rush to get away from the German Army who must have beaten us, otherwise we would not be running with our tails between our legs.

Self-preservation had taken over and our sad column of exiles had become spread out and disjointed, united only by wanting to get to Bir el Gubi and not to be taken prisoner. Our section had assumed a rear guard position to defend our miserable retreat with the 6-Pounder anti-tank guns if tanks or other enemy armoured vehicles attacked.

Tyre blow outs were an ever present risk. Changing them quickly became an imperative for survival.

(George Frame collection)

It was late in an afternoon when we stopped, exhausted, for a break. There were five 6-Pounders attached to trucks with eight trucks and perhaps fifty or so chaps in our rag tag group. The rest of the column was ahead of us because we had to stop at one point to replace a tyre on one of the trucks. We expected some stragglers may still be coming along behind.

The water for the brew had not yet boiled when all hell broke loose. Bullets were flying everywhere. I saw one poor fellow get hit and he went down like a sack of potatoes. The firing came from a low ridge that was close by. Confusion and panic took over as we scrambled to our trucks to get away. Some of our chaps began firing back but that was useless. I heard the zip zip as bullets flew past me and I found myself saying 'Don't hit me' as I ran to the truck. I clambered into the driver's seat, started the engine and while other chaps clambered aboard I let go the clutch. The lads were running to catch up so I slowed down briefly to let more get in the back. I instinctively drove away from the direction the bullets were coming from.

The other trucks were driving off in all directions. I learned later that several other trucks set off back along the route we had come from and had been ambushed. Those not killed would have been captured.

In the mayhem I drove like a mad man towards a series of low mounds with bullets whizzing past. One chap in the back was hit, but not fatally. I came over a small rise to see, with one hell of a fright, that right in front of me was a low stone wall. In the middle of nowhere a disused ramshackle dwelling for God's sake! I had no time to think so I smashed the truck through the wall hoping that the truck would not be disabled. There was an almighty bang as the truck hit the wall which fortunately gave way. I then turned sharply into what looked to me then like a dry river bed which it couldn't have been. I was shaking like a leaf in a storm and found myself shouting at the truck not to stop. I did not know if I had damaged the tyres or radiator or the sump or all of them when I smashed through the wall. I was expecting the bloody truck to stall at any time.

We got away, eventually linking up with some other stragglers. Walter was with them. Walter and I hugged each other. After the elation of meeting up had past we both worried where Taffy was, hoping he was not dead and that he would pitch up when we re-joined the others. Once we regrouped it seemed we had lost several of our trucks and two of the 6-Pounders, plus 20 or so chaps. But they could have been anywhere. When we found out later that Taffy was missing both Walter and I were very down. We did not know if he was lying dead or wounded at the ambush site, captured or if he was somewhere else trying to get back.

I discovered, a long time later, that Taffy ended up as a POW, transported to Tunisia, then by sea to Italy and marched northwards as the Allied forces advanced through Italy. He was lucky to survive that ordeal. He ended up in a German POW camp that was eventually liberated by the British. We met up in Salisbury after the war ended and shared time reminiscing, although Taffy carried a dark anger with him. On the forced marches up Italy the treatment metered out to the POW's was harsh with the weak and sick either shot or left in the snow to die. Although he never said it I sensed he may have felt that we abandoned him that day, but he had jumped into a truck that set off in the wrong direction and was captured. There was nothing Walter or I could have done to prevent that from happening.

The CO ordered us to head towards Al Adem to link up with the South Africans that he thought would be there. Trucks that had engine problems or ran short of petrol along the way were abandoned and were set alight. Water and food were also short so had to be rationed. We were all exhausted from both physical and emotional exertion.

Along the way we came across several abandoned Valentines tanks and supply trucks. They were not damaged and no evidence of any tank battle was there. They had run out of fuel. We stopped to scavenge whatever we could find. However when a cloud of dust was seen to the west of us, the CO decided it must be the Germans or Italians and we immediately set off. We set the supply trucks alight.

I have always been a positive sort of bloke, but at that time I felt that we were on our last legs and it would all be over soon – either dead or captured. We looked like a defeated bunch of misfits trying to escape a far stronger, more organised army. I think that this sentiment was shared amongst all of us.

When we got the news that Al Adem was in German hands our plans changed dramatically. I wondered what had happened to the South Africans who had been there. Had they been wiped out, retreated or moved to Tobruk? That news meant the Germans were between us and Tobruk. The CO ordered us to high tail it east towards the Egyptian border and then on to Mersa Matruth. As we understood it, the whole Eighth Army was now in retreat. Everyone for themselves to get back to Egypt.

What a bloody mess!

The retreat was chaotic and our chaps were taking a hiding.

(George Frame collection)

My mind focused on how to get out of this Libyan Desert and into Egypt. On reflection, it was an irrational thought process, but to me, at that time,

Egypt seemed to be safe, whereas Libya was not. It was not that long ago in actual time, but it seemed a lifetime ago, that we had been at Mersa Matruth and all excited that the Germans were beaten. Now we were racing back again with our tails between our legs, fearing the Germans would beat us there.

The concern whether we had enough fuel to get us back became acute. Water was running out. Food was minimal. In fact it started to look like we may well have to surrender to whomever was pursuing us or die in this desolate place from lack of water. Salvation came when another column of stranglers arrived with a plentiful stock of fuel and water.

We were indeed very lucky that day.

The light of dawn was breaking the Eastern horizon when the tin that was half full of water began to boil. The chaps were folding up the tarpaulins and packing them into the trucks together with our sleeping blankets. It had been a bitterly cold night and it seemed to me as if the temperature fell sharply since the light of another day cracked the distant skyline. I sat on a fuel can to remove the paper I had packed into my boots. It acted as a form of insulation in an attempt to keep my feet warm. I had to protect the paper with my life so the others would not use it to light the evening fire.

I was carefully stashing the paper after putting my boots back on having noticed that there was a hole in my one of my socks and wondering how I was going to mend it, when I first heard the sound. Moments before that I noticed that others had stopped what they were doing to listen. Soon we all were straining to hear. Occasions like this reminded me of the Meerkats in Southern Africa. They would go around busily searching for food or moving about the bush, always with one on guard duty. Then all of a sudden they would stop what they were doing, rise up on their hind quarters and listen and look. Comical to see really but there was a seriousness about their action. Life or death!

We began asking each other what the sound was. Then, as the chatter grew, our Officer told us to shut up. He and another chap clambered up to stand on top of one of the trucks and began searching the expanse of desert with their binoculars. The noise was coming from the West which was still cloaked in darkness and that's where we thought our chaps were and definitely we knew the Germans would be. The sky in the east began to turn orange with a light blue hue that quickly spread westward. On reflection, with the light behind us, our silhouette would have been clear to anyone west of us. And it was.

The CO continued to search through his binoculars when we saw a flash in the darkness. The bang when the shell exploded fifty to seventy yards or so short of where we were gave us a start. So now we knew the Germans were coming and they had seen us.

The two atop the truck jumped down, the CO shouting to us to get out of there. I was well ahead of that thought process and was already clambering into the driver seat of my truck. I immediately pumped the accelerator pedal and turned the key, hoping that the bloody engine would start. It did and I yelled out my window to the others to get on board.

The second explosion seemed a lot closer than the first. Of all the vehicles we had, mine was the furthest away. The CO clambered into the passenger seat and suggested quite emotionally, using a choice of expletives, that we should get going. I let go the clutch and the truck lurched forward. Thankfully the rear wheels got immediate traction and we were off. We had learned to ensure the trucks back wheels were not parked on soft ground. If they were the risk of them sinking under the weight of the truck could mean some digging to get the truck moving. The other trucks followed close behind.

The cat and mouse game of the desert war continued.

It was hard to see ahead with the dim light but luckily the terrain was quite flat. I heard another explosion. It looked like the shell had exploded to our right, near the third truck behind us. The CO stood up and peered out backwards. He leant back to get his binoculars and then began to scan for the enemy. The next plume of sand and smoke was close to us on our left. He yelled at me. "Right hand down. Right hand down man!"

I turned the truck right. The next explosion, although to our left, was further away. It seemed we were expanding the gap between us and the Germans. Eventually he sat down muttering that it was a close run thing. He said that the outline of the tanks he saw were not the same as those we had encountered previously. They looked bigger and boxier. I couldn't have cared less. All I wanted to do was get as far away from them as fast as possible. Then disaster struck! The front left tyre blew and the truck veered off leftwards. I must have gone over a sharp rock. Realising we had a puncture and the tyre was flat, I applied the brakes gently so as not to dig the wheel into the soil. We came to a stop as the sun broke the horizon and light quickly filled the dark void of the desert. The others stopped behind my truck. The CO clambered up onto the bonnet with his binoculars. Meanwhile I had jumped out of the cab and together with another chap we rushed to unpack the tool kit for the jack and wheel nut spanner. Two others were fetching the spare wheel. A quick decision had to be made. Do we change the tyre or abandon and burn the truck?

The CO yelled down that it would not take the Germans that long before they would be in firing range.

"How quick can you change the bloody wheel Frame?" he asked.

"Five minutes," I replied.

"We may not have that long …"

The decision not to stand and fight it out was made. The range of the tanks was greater than the range of our 6-Pounder. Now it was crunch time for the choice between replacing the tyre in time, abandon the truck, or get blown to smithereens by the Germans.

We heard the whoosh of the shell before it exploded in a small sand dune. The next one was likely to hit us. The CO ordered the other trucks to move on and they wasted no time to get moving once he got aboard one of them. We were on our own.

As another lad tightened the wheel nuts I clambered aboard without lowering the jack. I had left the engine running. The other chap jumped on the running board of the truck. Gear in, clutch out and the truck lurched. I'm not certain where the next shell landed. The accuracy of the German tankers was renowned and so I can speculate that the next round or the one after would surely have hit the truck had we not moved off.

We changed the tyre in three minutes!

Fear had our blood pumping. I drove like a man possessed chasing the dust rising from the trucks ahead of us and not looking back. After a short while we caught up and didn't stop running until later that afternoon. When we stopped we laughed hysterically at our skill at avoiding the Germans. Or was it just good fortune that day?

We made the dash for Sidi Omar and then onwards towards Mersa Matruth without any further contact with the enemy on the ground. Thankfully we did not see any enemy aircraft either.

I had never seen so many tanks, guns and trucks when we came into the vicinity of Mersa Matruth. The whole Eighth Army seemed to be there! We were able to rest up briefly, restock ourselves with water, food and fuel, but we were soon on our way along the coast road eastwards. The big retreat was in full swing.

We heard that the Boys in Blue had accidently bombed our own chaps near Mersa Matruth, killing many. Apparently it took place not long after we had passed through there so I suppose we could count ourselves fortunate it was not us. With all the confusion I was surprised such things did not happen more often.

The news that Tobruk had fallen several days before and that a lot of our chaps had either been killed or taken prisoner was a big kick in the guts to our morale. It seemed that the South Africans, Indians and New Zealanders were taking the brunt of the hiding in this war in the desert.

Did you know?

After the rout of the Eighth Army at Mersa Matruh by the Afrika Korps which pushed the whole army back into Egypt, a panic spread throughout Egypt and in particular in the British army headquarters in Cairo. This period became known as 'The Flap' and on what was called "Ash Wednesday" confidential papers were burned in all British controlled buildings fearing the imminent arrival of the Axis into the city.

Defensive positions were hurriedly built west of Alexandria as considerable areas of the Nile delta were flooded.

Meanwhile the Italian leader, Mussolini, flew to Libya and prepared for a triumphal entry into Cairo.

The CO told us that we were going to the south east of Al Alamein and once again we would be in a reserve force. We understood that Al Alamein was where the top brass had decided to make the final stand against Rommel because it was the narrowest point along the coastal strip with the sea to the north and a big depression, called Qattarra, to the south. That would allow a massing of our forces while preventing Rommel pulling another southern flanking move as he had just done. The gap between the sea and the depression was not that wide so our forces could be concentrated to defend it better. If Rommel broke through at Al Alamein then his army would take Cairo and Egypt would be lost to the Empire.

If you blinked you would miss Al Alemein. I could not even recall passing it when we originally were travelling from Cairo westwards to join the Eighth Army. I nearly missed it again on the way past going east. There was a railway siding and nothing else really other than a flat sandy desert. When we got past Al Alemein we turned south and once again journeyed into the vastness of the desert.

Chapter Eight

After the chaotic rush back from Libya the Eighth Army had set up a defensive line between the sea and the Depression. Anti-tank mines had been laid all along the defensive line together with barbed wire fences. Once again there had been that awful lull as both sides took stock, re-armed preparing to engage in battle.

We had settled into an uneasy rear guard defensive position south of a rugged rocky ridge line, but north of the Depression. A lot of activity had been going on along the ridge building stronger defences in case Rommel broke through the southern defences and tried to push northwards as he had done at Gazala. The Free French, those who had extricated themselves from Bir Hacheim, were to our south closer to the Depression. South Africans were apparently to our north west.

Our CO told us that Rommel may well try to outflank the defensive line and this meant an attack in the south where we were situated with the 7th Armoured Division. Our role would be to push back the German tanks if they broke through. The reserve forces, of which we were part, were the last line of defence for Egypt and I held little hope for Egypt if the enemy did break through.

We had resupplied ourselves with fuel, food and water, plus plenty of shells. We had cleaned the anti-tank guns and serviced the trucks. Now our fate, and that of the Empire, was about to unfold in front of us, or so we thought.

We had been in our location south east of Al Alemein for quite some time when the news that our reserve unit were to get new truck-mounted anti-tank guns. This news gave us a boost given we were all pretty down, feeling defeated, wondering how we would stop Rommel.

The CO selected some of us to travel to a depot near Al Alamein to fetch these trucks and to restock on supplies. I was the driver of one of the two trucks that set off early one morning. It was a relief actually to be able to get away. I felt the tension within me lift soon after we set off, probably because we were on a mission rather than the monotony of what we had been doing these past few weeks. Doing nothing and waiting to be attacked played havoc on one's nerves.

The journey was proving to be uneventful when we stopped for a brew up at midday. It was only a short stop before we set off so as to get to the depot before dusk. I was driving the second truck in the two truck convoy and was in a sort of mesmerized state watching the back of the lead truck with its dust clouds coming up from the back wheels. The heat of the day was making me feel sleepy.

All of a sudden the canvass covering the truck ahead ripped open and the truck swerved off to the right. Then I heard a wooosh as a plane shot past. I slammed on the break forgetting the clutch. The truck staggered to a stop. Walter, who was in the cab with me, shouted, "What the bloody hell was that George?"

I could barely see the plane speeding away when I looked out the side window. It was not that easy to see because it was painted in a sandy camouflage. It was a bloody 109!

Looking back to the other truck which had stopped, I noticed chaps debussing and running. Walter was already out of the cab and when I opened the door I saw the chaps from the back of my truck jumping off and making a dash. I looked back to see where the plane had gone but was unable to locate it. I could hear it though and the sound was getting louder rather than fainter.

I ran around the front of the truck and away from it intending to put the truck between me and the plane which, by the sound of it, was coming back. I heard the clatter of gun fire above the noise of the plane's engine. Scared, not knowing what actually was happening behind me, I just ran for my life. Walter and a few others were running ahead of me and to my right. I heard the whack! whack! which I discovered afterwards were bullets smashing into the truck before I saw puffs of sand in a streaking row moving fast past me and towards the other chaps. Walter turned right and was missed by a hairs breath. I dived into a small depression in the ground.

The plane soared overhead. I had my head buried in the sand with my hands over my head so I did not see the plane again. Once the sound of the plane's engines faded I lifted myself out of the dip and looked around. Chaps were staggering back towards the trucks. There was no smoke so I thought the pilot must have been a poor shot to have missed the trucks and how lucky we had been. I went over to Walter, who was sitting on the ground, to see if he had been hit. He was okay but was shaken up. All he could say was "That bastard wanted to kill me George!"

The picture back at the trucks was bleak. The lead truck was badly shot up and was unusable. But worse news was that one chap in the back was dead and another had been shot. A bullet had virtually severed his foot and there was blood everywhere. He was in shock, shaking and sweating.

My truck was okay. We loaded everyone into the one truck including the poor dead chap and the lad with the bad wound, who was sedated. I drove off as fast as we could towards the coast. We got to the depot in the late afternoon. We were told later on that the chap who was wounded lost his leg below the knee. At least he was sent home alive.

The incident with the 109 had an unintended consequence. It delayed us at the depot for a few days while a replacement truck was sourced.

Conference in the desert (George Frame Collection)

Rumours abounded that Auchinleck had been sacked. Auchinleck was the commander of the Eighth Army who had taken us from Egypt to Libya and now back to Egypt. The news that he had been removed came as no real consequence to us. We just hoped that whomever replaced him could do a better job of things to win this bloody war in the desert so we could all go home. But more importantly, the rumour was that Churchill was here. The story flying around was that he had come to take charge of the army himself. I didn't know what to make of that news.

Churchill visited Egypt in July 1942. (George Frame collection)

We were unexpectedly given two days leave when our CO was summoned to meet with the top brass at Alexandria. Beer and food and a good night's sleep were top of mind! We soon found a watering hole full of Australians. Once it was ascertained we were Rhodesian and not British we fitted right in and got plastered together.

When I mentioned that Churchill was supposedly in Alexandria to take over the command of the Eighth Army I was most surprised to hear a barrage of abuse from the Australians. I soon realised they were pretty belligerent towards Churchill, a result from the First World War.

The crew letting off steam in Alexandra. George at back.

(George Frame collection)

Central Railway Station in Alexandria. (George Frame collection)

The Gardens at Alexandria. (George Frame collection)

The two days passed in a blur and we returned to the depot in a very sad, hungover state where we collected the two new mounted anti-tank gun trucks and a replacement truck for the one the 109 had shot up. The array of military equipment and new tanks and field guns was impressive. There were rows of the Grant tanks. I also saw my first Sherman tanks. They looked terrific. Their engine made a thumping noise and I thought they must use an awful lot of fuel and wondered how the fuel supply to these monsters would work out if we ever made it back into Libya.

The new tanks that would turn the war from defeat to victory.

(George Frame collection)

Did you know?

The industrial might of the USA swung the pendulum against Nazi Germany. The North African campaign was essentially a tank battleground and the arrival of the Grant tank was a defining moment.

The American M3 medium tank was particularly distinctive from most other tanks. It had a 75 mm gun as its main weapon which was mounted on a sponson on the side of the vehicle, while a 37 mm gun was mounted in the turret. The British equipped their design with a lower turret to that of the US variants. The British tanks were called "Grants" or "General

Grants", and also required one less crew member than those used in the US army.

Specifications for this tank were: 75 mm M2 or M3 gun, 37 mm M5 or M6 gun, two .30-calibre Browning machine-guns. The armour was 51 mm. Power plant: Twin General Motors 60446 series 71 diesel.

The new mounted anti-tank guns were a great advantage for manoeuvrability, but they were still 2 pounders.

A mid-day brew underway. (George Frame collection)

We joined a large convoy heading towards the Front with the intention to veer off back to our unit south of Ruweisat Ridge. We were most fortunate to be with that convoy because during that time Winston Churchill arrived. It was a one in a million opportunity to have this great man in the presence of the chaps. His mere presence seemed to create a huge positive energy that rippled through all those present. However I did wonder what the Australians who were in that group thought.

Winston Churchill greeted troops in the desert before the battle of Al Alamein

(George Frame collection)

Emotionally I felt much better when we set off to re-join our own unit than how I had been feeling for months. The other chaps felt much the same. It was quite remarkable how one man's presence could have such an impact. But, at that moment, I just did not know what we were going back to.

Did you know?

Churchill had battled to get the United States of America to join the war. The losses and reversals in North Africa did not help him in that endeavour. He travelled by plane to the Middle East en route to meet Stalin. This was a very risky move given the dangers that abounded in southern Europe and North Africa. He travelled aboard a Liberator bomber flown by a young Bill Vanderkloot from Illinois. So noisy, Churchill was only able to communicate with others on board by hand written notes.

Churchill wrote to his wife from Cairo, "I intend to see every important unit in this army, both back and front, and make them feel the vast consequences which depend upon them and the superb honours which may be theirs."

He felt Britain needed generals who had fire in their bellies and those he had chosen had failed the test. His purge of the generals in the desert was treated with unsurprising caution in the British Government. Auchinleck was bitter of his sacking and held a grudge against Churchill for the rest of his life.

Churchill described September and October 1942 as the most anxious months of the entire war.

We were told that a General Montgomery had been made the commander of the Eighth Army. He was Irish. The Irish had a reputation for being 'hot heads' and I wondered if he was one of them and, if so, what catastrophes he may take us all into.

Nothing much happened for weeks after we returned other than those chaps who were allocated the mobile anti-tank vehicles practiced using them. I was not allocated to the two teams to operate the mounted anti-tank guns. I had mixed feelings about that. While the concept of having a mobile gun that one could fire at the enemy from and then get away fast, if the situation became desperate, sounded great. The gun was still only a two pounder which I felt was just about useless against the German Panzer. The anti-tank gun I was attached to was a 6 pounder and while it was immobile once unattached from the truck I felt it offered more of a chance to knock out the enemy armour. The down side was the time required to disengage it from the truck and set it up and the time to attach it to a truck to get away in a desperate situation. The alternative was to abandon the gun. On balance I reconciled myself that I was better off with the gun we had.

The CO gave me a promotion to Corporal and so I was now in charge of the 6 pound anti-tank gun, truck and crew. The prospect of that did not enthral me, but the improvement in pay did.

Then one early morning as a slight sliver of light crept up from the horizon the sound of guns shattered the silence.

The date was the end of August 1942.

A few days before that fateful morning we had observed many tanks moving around. Our Valentine's and Humber Mk II seemed no match for the German Panzers. The chaps in them must have felt vulnerable and I thought they must be so brave to go into battle against the odds that were stacked against them surviving. The Crusader and Matilda tanks were marginally better, while the new American Grant's appeared best equipped to take on the Panzer's.

Hearing the enemy artillery fire was the signal that Rommel was attacking us. I awoke to that rumble and while it seemed to be a distance away from us I was immediately alert and got my chaps up. When dawn crept upon us our CO told us that Rommel was attacking with his armour through the extreme southern part of the defensive line.

We could hear the guns going off in the west and sometimes they seemed far closer than they turned out to be. Seeing our Boys in Blue flying overhead gave us encouragement. I wished them much success in cleaning up the enemy. Surprisingly we did not see the German or Italian air force.

Tension was high. As the day progressed the noise of the gun fire became more distant and it came more from towards the ridge. We gathered that the Free French would have incurred the brunt of the offensive as they were towards the southern end of the defence line but were still unaware of what was actually happening.

We were informed later that day that Rommel had broken through with his tanks and had turned north towards the ridge line where our forces were dug in. Because he had not ventured too far eastwards we had not been engaged. The CO thought we may be asked to move up north to out flank his rear, but no orders to that effect came through that day.

It soon started to look like a stalemate had developed and thankfully Rommel's forces had not been able to break through the ridge defences. Orders came through to harass the German tanks as they were withdrawing towards the south back towards where they had broken through. We pulled the anti-tank guns out from the dug in positions, took off the netting and loaded all the munitions back onto the trucks. As soon as this was done we moved off in a westerly direction and into the dusk.

I was glad when the dawn arrived the following day so that we could at least see ahead, but there was very poor visibility. We were all on edge, expecting the enemy at any moment. In these circumstances one gets a heavy feeling in the base of the stomach, the adrenalin pumps and skin sweats. Senses are at breaking point to pick up any movement and sound. After a while though tiredness sweeps over in waves. Then, of all things to happen, a bloody sand storm swept through showering us with sand, reducing visibility to a few yards. That only made us more tense. Not being able to see the horizon when a battle is raging is quite frightening. The enemy tanks could be on top of us before we could even see them.

We expected to see action and when we did finally see tanks in the distance it was rather a surreal sensation. This was it! Fear disappeared and survival mode kicked in. We had to kill them or be killed. How they had got through the mine field and avoided the artillery was a mystery. How they had fought their way to the ridge was surprising, but that did not matter. The incoming shells were our main concern.

We hurriedly deployed our guns and fired constantly and, in my new role of looking through the field glasses to direct my chaps with direction and trajectory, I was able to see the action taking place. The tanks fired towards our position and initially their shells fell short. We hit one tank and its tread unravelled. It stopped and I was able to see its crew scramble out and high tail it back. Then a tank took a direct hit from another anti-tank gun and went up like a fire cracker. Soon thereafter the enemy tanks backed off. We stopped firing at them.

But that reprieve was short lived and it was not long before they came in once again.

The situation was dire because if any tanks overran the anti-tank gun defence at any point it was probable all of us would be done for. When some enemy tanks looked like they would outflank us the CO ordered the mobile anti-tank gun trucks to deal with them. They dashed off to engage these tanks. Sadly during that engagement one of our mobile anti-tanks trucks received a hit.

We held the enemy at bay until the Grant tanks entered the battle then we ceased firing. The situation on the battlefield looked confused with dust swirling around reducing visibility. I could catch glimpses of tanks moving in all directions firing at each other. It was fascinating to see how manoeuvrable they were in pitched battle. Moving forward, backwards and swivelling around. Amongst it all there were tanks ablaze pouring thick smoke into the sky.

When the enemy armour finally retreated the relief was tremendous. Some chaps whooped and hollered more to release nervous energy than for joy. I felt totally exhausted and thankful the bastards did not get through. But the news about the loss of our chaps when their mobile anti-tank truck was hit it made us all feel very sad indeed. We liked to think their action prevented the tanks coming up behind us. Their bodies were retrieved before the sun set. Thankfully I did not have to take part in that.

Destroyed British 2 pounder anti-tank gun. (George Frame Collection)

We heard that the New Zealand soldiers had a rough day of it. The New Zealanders were a tough bunch who had fought hard in all the battles. Having them on our side was comforting.

That night the drone of planes could be heard constantly. Looking west into the blackness of the night I could see flashes over the horizon. I hoped our boys were bombing the hell out of Rommel. I did not really sleep, only cat naps, so by dawn I was really tired. Expecting another pounding, we were on edge. I gulped down the tea but was not able to eat anything. The pit of my stomach felt like led. Any food would have come straight back up. While we could hear gun fire in the distance and our planes flew overhead a few times, we were to be spared from any action that day. Rommel's forces had withdrawn and we could breathe easy once more.

I was not in the best of shape. I had been struggling to get any decent rest, my appetite was not that good and I had lost weight in recent weeks, looking like skin and bones with my uniform hanging loosely.

Nervous tension filled our days. (George Frame collection)

During the next two months there was a lot of troop and armour movement and we were part of that activity. We just moved about. There were mine fields all over the place so one had to be very wary not to inadvertently wander into one. Whenever there was a lull in action, like that we were experiencing, any activity that took place always led to rumours and heightened anxiety so at that time the rumour mill was in full swing.

George takes time to shave in the middle of nowhere. (George Frame collection)

Orders came through that we were to redeploy further south east and for a few weeks we wandered around the vast desert landscape. When we were close to the Depression at one stage, I hoped that we could go and see what the feature was like. Unfortunately we never got to it.

Mine fields scattered over the defensive line with crude barbed wire fencing.

(George Frame collection)

On a few occasions, as we roved around, we observed several concentrations of tanks. At one point we drove past chaps working on a pipeline which we understood was to bring fuel to the front line. That night, when we were having dinner, we discussed the pipeline and all agreed it was a dumb thing to do as it was exposed and the Germans would probably bomb it.

A few days later we came across wooden structures being erected. There were dozens of them. They were being constructed in the shape of tanks. This both confused and worried us. Were we so short of tanks that we now built dummy ones to bluff Rommel? The confusion that arose from that thought process had a demoralising effect on us. We started to think that when Rommel made his next attack we probably would be done for. After having Generals lead the Eighth Army to the brink of winning this war a year earlier, to end up with our back against the wall in the last defence before Alexandria and Cairo and with all the death and destruction in between, I shared the despondency that many chaps had in our leadership. Years later I read that these wooden tanks were a smart tactic used to lure Rommel to believe the Eighth Army had far more tanks than they actually did and they were spread the length of the defensive line when in actual fact, the real tanks were being concentrated north for the big push through.

A game of darts to relieve tension. (George Frame collection)

I thought we should do more practice in hooking up and unhooking our gun because a fear I had was being overrun by the enemy and bayonetted. I thought that if we became proficient at attaching the gun to the truck we would be able to get away faster and therefore avoid being overrun. The chaps complained a bit, but I insisted.

Every now and again the enemy planes would attack and then the AA guns would blast away. Whenever one of their planes went down it was a relief. Occasionally we would go and have a look. Whenever we saw our Boys in Blue flying overhead that did make us feel safer. I thought that at least they would stop the Stuka and 109's from coming at us because being dug in and stationary we were sitting ducks for an air attack.

Search lights (George Frame Collection)

Downed enemy plane being guarded by Tommy. (George Frame collection)

On this particular day we were on another boring patrol as we had done each day for weeks. It had been particularly cold. Out in the desert it sometimes felt like we could freeze to death at night especially when the wind cut right through. Soon after we had packed up we came across several tanks and other vehicles close to the mine field. The CO had us stop and the word was soon out that Monty was here. I could not believe this. The Eighth Army Commander less than half a mile from the Front rather than hiding behind a desk back in Alexandria! At that instant, I changed my mind about this chap. It was strange how my spirit and those of the other lads lifted and how, once again, one man could have that impact.

Lieutenant General Bernard Montgomery (2nd from left) at the front line near the Murassib Depression south of Al Alamein.

(George Frame collection)

Did you know?

Born in London in 1887 Bernard Montgomery was one of nine children of Reverend Henry Montgomery and his wife Maud. Before his father was made Bishop of Tasmania in 1889 his early years were in Northern Ireland. His childhood was harsh especially when living in the remote Tasmanian colony. His mother was not averse to dishing out beatings regularly. At the age of fourteen the family returned to Britain and he attended St. Paul's School before entering the Royal Military Academy at Sandhurst where he graduated as a second lieutenant.

He was knighted and promoted to General after Al Alamein.

Monty handing out awards for bravery in battle. (George Frame collection)

A bizarre occurrence happened one day when, in the distance, we heard what sounded like bagpipes. It couldn't be? Then the sound got louder and to our amazement we saw a large contingent of soldiers marching along behind a pipe band! I must say the sound of those bagpipes sent chills down my spine. That evening we mused that the mad Scots would either cause the Germans to surrender to stop the noise, or they would probably beat them to pulp with their bagpipes.

The Scots marching to war. (George Frame collection)

Our crew relaxing in the desert. (George Frame collection)

During mid-October we noticed that there were considerable armour and troop redeployments taking place. We received orders to position ourselves behind the artillery that was being deployed by the 7th Armoured Division. The 44th Infantry Division was deployed at the Front. We were in the reserve force once again.

Real tanks as opposed to the fake ones built from wood! (George Frame collection)

The CO explained to us that there was to be an offensive against Rommel's forces along the Front and our mission was to defend the rear if enemy armour penetrated the advance. I thought that with all the movement of tanks and vehicles including the artillery the main push was likely to be where we were in the south. The speculation was that we would emulate the strategy of Rommel by attacking in the south then turn north to outflank and encircle. Many of us had become expert strategists and I was no exception!

Did you know?

The Second battle of El Alamein that took place between 23rd October and 11 November 1942 was the defining battle of the North African campaign and towards the final defeat of Rommel and his Afrika Korps. It was the first of the victories the Allied forces would inflict on Nazi Germany. The command of the Eighth Army had passed to Montgomery after the sacking of Auchinleck and the death of his replacement Lieutenant-General William Gott in a plane crash on his way to assume command.

Rommel had 116,000 men, 550 tanks, 190 armoured cars, 550 artillery and 500 anti-tank guns and around 450 serviceable aircraft at his disposal. Montgomery was fortunately resupplied and had 195,000 men, over 1,000 tanks, 450 armoured cars, 550 serviceable planes, around 900 artillery and 1,500 anti-tank guns.

This battle was brutal claiming around 55,000 German and Italian men killed, wounded or captured, the loss of around 500 tanks, 260 guns and with 85 aircraft lost.

Montgomery lost 14,000 men killed, wounded or missing, around 500 tanks, 110 guns and 90 aircraft lost.

When the orders came through that we were to be ready that night for something big, I became very apprehensive. My thoughts fled to my darling Lorraine who I felt had slipped away from me. Was I ever going to see her again? How I hoped she would remember me and the love I held for her long after I was dead. I hoped though that I would not end my life sprawled out in this dreadful desert. I don't think that the letters I wrote to my parents and Lorraine that evening were ever posted given the confusion of the next few weeks.

The CO read out a message that General Montgomery had sent to us all. He said to his army that we must have a desire to kill Germans and that included their chaplains even on a Sunday. We were to knock the Germans out of Africa. That we were to kill chaplains on a Sunday was a strange thing to say and I suppose had we heard this directly from the General's mouth it may have had more impact, but coming out of the CO's mouth it lacked the punch. I wondered why the Italians were not included in the speech which only referred to the Germans. The Italians were also the enemy. They may not be the best fighters in this conflict, but they could still pull a trigger on a gun to kill or wound us.

We understood that somewhere south of our position were the Free French while the New Zealanders, South Africans and Australians were up north. The Germans were apparently everywhere. It was suggested the Italian army was opposite our location.

Unable to sleep, worrying about what lay ahead, my thoughts raced back home to my childhood. The wonderful freedom I had enjoyed exploring the bush with my African friends was idyllic. When the Msasa trees turned a burned orange in spring to flood the countryside with colour that contrasted with those magnificent granite boulders I felt excited. The bush hummed with its own unique sound, being alive with birds and animals. Then in the winter months the stark brown of the grasses contrasted with the granite to bring its own beauty.

Msasa Tree in Rhodesia

(George Frame collection)

This place that we were in now was so different. Lifeless. And ironically it was very easy to also become lifeless. One bullet, a land mine or a shell from a tank or artillery would do that. A lifeless place that wanted to suck the life out of those people who were there summed up the scene.

Typical desert scene (George Frame collection)

Of course I thought of my family and wondered what they would be doing. Mother, at the Bulawayo home, trying to keep the house clean and cooking over the wood fire stove. She had done so much on her own to make a home for us given dad was always away at the mines. I wondered how often she thought of me and whether she was getting my letters. I hoped she was not worrying about me though, but suspected she must be. The confused news must be getting home that we were winning one day and loosing this bloody war the next. I imagined my father up in Northern Rhodesia on the mine. I suspect he thought less about how I was doing because he would be busy working long hours, but I hoped he would occasionally think of me.

Harold, my older brother, was working as an accounts clerk in Bulawayo. I wondered what he thought about the news they must be getting about this desert war. I had a standoff relationship with Harold for some reason. I think when we were younger, because he was my older brother, he had felt I should listen to him and when I didn't he became petulant. I preferred the outdoors and he didn't. When we went to a British boarding school in Lancaster as young boys, thousands of miles from our home, he did not really look out for me and rather chose to distance himself from his younger brother. I guess we all were trying to fit in to the rigid English grammar school way of life and being colonials didn't help us at all. It was easy to pick on us for being different so it was important to just fit in so as not to be picked on or bullied. I think he had a tougher time there than I did in that regard.

Douglas, my younger brother, was becoming an engineer, so he was probably fully occupied in his career prospects. I used to pick on Douglas for fun and now I regretted that. He was so easy to wind up though. My favourite thing to do was to mess his hair whenever I could. It drove him nuts. The other mean thing I had done was to turn my pet monkey against him. What I did to get that response was every time Douglas came near the monkey I would pinch its tail. It related the pinch to Douglas. It got to the stage that whenever Douglas came into its sight the monkey would go after him. Once the monkey bit poor Douglas which was not in the overall plan.

Then my thoughts of darling Lorraine. How I wanted so much to get back to South Africa and marry her. I worried that perhaps she had moved on. How was I to know what she had decided to do? After all we only knew each other for a few weeks. At times I struggled to picture her in my mind. Perhaps it was not to be after all.

The lads who were with me were also very anxious. We tried to talk and crack a joke but nothing seemed funny and so we ended up in silence, each in our own world of private thoughts. It was hard to encourage them when I was downcast myself. I did however say that we had to stick together to get through this, look out for each other and we just had to do what was necessary. I am not sure if that helped them or not.

The sky was glorious, filled with millions of stars that night. The moon shone in the distance making the scene very peaceful. There was only a light breeze. It was cold. We could hear the tanks and other vehicles moving around behind us, getting ready for the action that was about to start.

When the artillery opened up, the night sky lit up. The flashes going off one after the other turned night into day. The sound was deafening. The bang following the flash of light from the gun turrets carried on over and over. This barrage began not long after we had our supper which was a surprise to me because we had expected the artillery to get going just before dawn. The poor bastards on the receiving end must be getting pounded to dust.

We could still hear the rumble of other artillery further to our north after the artillery near us stopped. The sound of big guns firing was replaced with the sound of tanks when our chaps in the 7^{Th} Armoured Division rumbled forward. Clouds of dust were stirred up and while it was still dark it gave off an eerie aspect. As we had speculated, it now appeared that the push against Rommel was going to be from the south and then, presumably once behind the enemy lines, thrust northwards to the coast. Hitting the Italians seemed a sensible start as they were undoubtedly the soft underbelly of the Axis.

A chap called Horrocks was the overall CO of the 7th. Our CO thought highly of him saying he was trusted to make sound judgemental decisions. Well now was the time to put that view to the test. Many chaps would die if he made a shambles of what had started.

It was not long before gun fire erupted ahead of us which we thought was from our tanks engaging the Italians. We listened and waited as the battle took shape. The anxiety was intense. We were going to be moving across the minefield soon. Seeing what land mines could do, I certainly did not relish the thought of entering the minefields. I had discovered the evening before that this operation was called Lightfoot because if we had to walk across the minefields we should walk lightly, so as not to set off the mines. The trouble was that we were in trucks pulling anti-tank guns!

Fragmented reports trickled back to our own CO as the dawn cracked the horizon behind us. Our chaps up front had not succeeded in crossing the minefields yet and were therefore exposed with the dawn. We understood everyone was now digging in at the Front. Our orders were to move closer to the Front to assist with defensive cover fire if required.

The closer we got the louder was the clatter of sporadic gun fire. The visibility was very poor due to the dust in the air. I could not see more than about a hundred yards or so ahead. During that day we waited for further orders listening to sporadic outbursts of gun fire. None was directed at our location. It did not feel like a major offensive was in progress.

When the boys in blue appeared our spirits soared.

(George Frame collection)

In the late afternoon the fighting at the Front increased with more intense gun fire. At one stage the Boys in Blue came in to attack the Italians.

Several Hurricanes and bombers flew back low to the ground dipping their wings to the soldiers on the ground. That indicated to us a successful sortie. It lifted our spirits somewhat.

Remarkably I got some sleep that night after nervous exhaustion set in. Walter told me the next morning that incoming shells had exploded quite close to our position, yet I had slept through it.

The offensive ground to a halt and the 7th withdrew. A lot of tanks had been destroyed. It was demoralising to think that perhaps the plans to break out had failed and actually the Germans would win this after all.

Days passed by and the 7th were directed to rapidly move north. That was certainly unexpected and caused speculation that Rommel had broken through our lines near the coast. We pulled out late that afternoon and drove towards Al Alamein not entirely knowing what we were going into, but dreading that it may be to the German break through and their push to Alexandria.

We drove through most of the night so by the next morning we were close to Al Alamein. The rumble of gun fire in the west was ever-present. We could see thick smoke rising in the distance. When we heard that the German air force had hit fuel dumps our spirits sank. Loosing fuel supply had become a critical aspect of who won any battle, especially for the tanks.

When the picture became clear our CO informed us that the 7th Armoured Division was being relocated to the coast as a reserve force and that the main thrust of our attack against the enemy was along the coast. Hearing that helped to relieve the tension that had built up amongst us thinking we were on the defensive. Not knowing what we were heading to was nerve racking. We were to hold a position south of Al Alamein behind the South African army group.

The air force was far more active in this location of the Front with both day and night attacks on the enemy. The 7th Armoured Division tanks and artillery started arriving in force to regroup near Al Alamein. They brought the news that the chaps in the south, where we had been, had not broken through the minefields and had suffered a lot of casualties. That was disappointing to hear.

We were hungry for information on what was happening at the Front, but the news was not always reliable. We heard that the Australians had been engaged in a brutal battle to our north west but had not broken through the German lines. The New Zealanders had suffered badly and also had not broken through. It seemed to us that this big offensive was becoming another stalemate and we could well lose it.

While we waited we made sure our equipment was in the best order possible, either for a rapid retreat to Cairo or a push to Tobruk!

The day we relocated further towards the coast the air force activity was huge with planes flying back and forth for many hours. We collectively hoped that they would do the job for us. The next day, before dawn, we heard the sound of artillery guns blasting away in the distance which alerted us to the possibility a major offensive was about to happen. But we were not entirely sure whose offensive it would be.

We got orders to prepare for action and immediately the whole Division began to mobilise towards the Front. Suppressing the anxiety of the situation, knowing that so many chaps had been killed over the past few days, was not easy when wondering if your number was going to be up in this next phase of battle. The Panzers were formidable and the 88mm flak guns used by the Germans could knock you out before you could even get close enough to fire back.

We manoeuvred ourselves towards the Front and went through the minefields agonisingly slowly. I was sitting in the passenger seat of our truck looking closely at the track ahead. The engineers had cleared the path placing markers for us to drive between, but there was always that lingering doubt about a rouge land mine left behind. Silly really as we were not the first to traverse across the minefield and if there had been any left, they would have already gone off.

Once we got through the minefield the scene confronting us was horrific. I thought I had seen the worst of it, but this was just horrible. We drove through carnage. The waves of smoke and stench of burned or burning bodies caught in the back of ones throat and I gagged a few times. Although it was bloody hot, I wrapped a scarf around my face and nose to reduce the smell. Bodies, swarms of flies, burned out tanks, guns, trucks, many still smouldering. The smoke and dust mingled together to make visibility poor. The images were haunting, tearing at the core of one's emotion. Very little was said. What on earth could be said for such slaughter?

Destroyed German 88mm flak gun and transport. (George Frame Collection)

Both seemingly intact and damaged equipment littered the landscape.

(George Frame collection)

Of course seeing this did not help me or our chaps feel any more confident that we were not going to be blown to bits at any minute. I think each of us hoped that if that moment came, our death would be instant and painless. We had seen our fellow soldiers writhing in agony with horrific wounds, stumps of remains of legs or arms or gaping holes in the body. Truly terrible agony.

After seeing the extent of the destruction, I wondered what could possibly be left of our tanks and of Rommel's army.

We were told Rommel was withdrawing along the coast. Our Division rolled westwards further to the south of the coast with what I later understood was a plan to encircle the German and Italians preventing them retreating back to Mersa Maruh.

We were moving at some speed when all of a sudden it set off!

Gun fire erupted some distance ahead of us as our tanks engaged the enemy and our orders were to quickly move forward and position ourselves to repel enemy tanks. We had no time to dig in. We unhitched the 6 pounder gun in record time and positioned ourselves for the battle. The CO informed us that our tanks had met stiff resistance from Italians. The plan was they would feint a withdrawal so as to draw the enemy tanks forward into a barrage from the anti-tank guns. Once again there were dust clouds surrounding the whole area making the visibility situation difficult for us. By the time we got set, the sound of tanks firing at each other was getting closer.

I was sweating profusely. My mind was trying to focus on the task at hand to stay alive. Walter smiled at me and said, "Let's give the bastards a right royal send-off George".

While looking through the binoculars, searching for a target, I thought briefly of Lorraine, hoping we would meet again in life rather than in spirit, which somehow helped me steady my nerves.

Our tanks withdrew through our lines, swirling dust clouds. The CO yelled something about being ready to engage, but I found it hard to hear much with the racket from the tank engines and the thumping of my heart in my ears.

The shape of a tank moving towards us emerged in the vision of the field glasses and I gave the direction to Walter. Our gun turret was lowered and we fired. The other anti-tank guns either side of us blasted. Our shot missed. I could see flashes in the dust cloud which told me the enemy tanks were firing back on us. Seeing what looked like red balls of fire hurtling towards us, and the whistle of the shells passing overhead, sent shivers down ones spine. Which one would hit us?

Left a touch and we fired again. The tank was hit and it stopped. I was not entirely sure if we had hit it or if was another gun. I searched for another target. We swivelled our gun and fired. Again a miss.

The barrage of fire from our anti-tank guns was consistent. I heard a loud explosion and searched through the field glasses to see where it came from. The turret on a tank had blown off. When the wind swirled and visibility was momentarily clear, I saw another tank hit and burst into fire. Its crew tried to escape. Seeing men on fire, flailing around in desperation to extinguish the flames burning their flesh is something I would not wish on my worst enemy.

We fired over and over hitting one other tank before the enemy withdrew. Our tanks then moved forward to engage them and we could hear the battle rage up ahead for quite some time. Our anti-tank section had not sustained any damage or casualties inflicted. I was glad it was the Italians that we engaged and not the Germans. The Italian tanks were not that good in comparison to either the German Panzer or our newer tanks and were no match to our 6 pounder anti-tank guns range and calibre.

When the dust cloud thinned we could observe the scene ahead. Many tanks were alight, dead Italian soldiers, smoke. Some chaps moved cautiously forward to investigate while we hitched up the gun and stored the ammunition, readying to move forward once again. Some gun fire erupted. Maybe it was our chaps shooting some enemy they came across. There was no time to bury the dead this day because the army was on the chase, having broken through the enemy line. That task would have to wait until later.

Later on that day we saw some trucks in the distance travelling parallel to us. Searching through his field glasses, the CO said they were Italian and ordered we fire at them. We did this with the mobile anti-tank guns, hitting one of the trucks which exploded. The others shot off southwards away from us to where the New Zealand force was so perhaps they got to clean up the Italian stragglers. We did not go to see what damage we had done as our objective was to get to the railway line to engage retreating enemy tanks or trucks. By this time we had the sense that the enemy were being routed and while the danger of being shot at was ever present our perception of the situation had changed positively over the past few hours.

We then turned northwards and we arrived at the railway line late that afternoon. The information we had was the enemy was in retreat towards Mersa Matruh. I remarked to our chaps how many more times would we pass through that dismal place before this dreadful war was ended.

The railway line was important to move equipment towards the front.

(George Frame collection)

At one point we saw a large column of prisoners being escorted by our chaps. They were Italians and looked in worse shape than we did, but at least now they were free from being killed in this battle ground. I learned afterwards that the Italians had been abandoned by the Germans in the retreat, hence the large numbers captured.

The end of their war – prisoners being marched away from the front lines

(George Frame collection)

The following day we came across abandoned tanks and trucks strewn in the desert. There were some 88mm guns abandoned which we had a look at. These were dreadfully accurate and deadly weapons which we were so pleased had not fired at us so far. The Germans must have run out of fuel.

Abandoned equipment – presumably from lack of fuel.

(George Frame Collection)

Several Grant tanks passed nearby churning up clouds of dust as they belted along. Every now and again gun fire erupted somewhere which always made one edgy. In the vast expanse of nothing that we were in, there were gullies, rocky outcrops and small hills, all which could hide an enemy planning an ambush.

Then, of all things to happen, it rained and with it the ground quickly turned into mud. Along with a few others, our truck and gun got bogged. We had to dig it out which was no easy task. Each time we seemed to get moving we got bogged again. One good thing was that I stood in the rain, in my underwear, to wash off the grime and dust. It felt glorious.

We received orders to quickly move west to support the tanks which had come across the German Panzers. Because we were bogged, by the time we arrived the battle was largely over. Many German tanks were ablaze and clearly they had been well and truly outdone by our chaps.

We did however engage a few trucks, some towing artillery pieces, with the mobile anti-tank guns and gun fire in a short exchange before they raced off into the expanse of the desert. My truck was hit with some rounds but thankfully not enough to disable it.

It was soon after that short exchange of fire that I started to get sharp stabbing pains which made me think I could have been hit by a bullet or shrapnel. I stripped off to have a look and the chaps had a good laugh when nothing was found other than I looked like a walking skeleton. I was having to tie my trousers with a piece of rope for them to stay up because I had lost a lot of weight.

George with fuel cans looking thin

(George Frame collection)

We went through the Haifaya Pass again. It didn't seem that long ago we had been rushing through it towards Cairo with our tails between our legs.

Rommel had retreated. Our chaps had not cut him off from escaping through the pass which meant another long slog back through Libya.

Our advancing army began to run out of fuel which raised this whole issue of supply again. It seemed to me that this desert war would never be won because when we went west it stretched our supply and when Rommel went east the same happened to him. I was convinced that the supply of fuel for the tanks would decide the result one way or the other.

We stopped near a place called Musaid on the Egypt / Libya border. I was grateful for the stop because I was not feeling well and needed to rest. But the supply trucks arrived soon enough and after a day's rest up we were on the move again, this time leaving the coast road and travelling inland.

On the way west we came across German burial grounds. Rows of distinctive crosses, some with the poor fellow's helmet attached. I was impressed that the Germans had time and consideration to respect their dead.

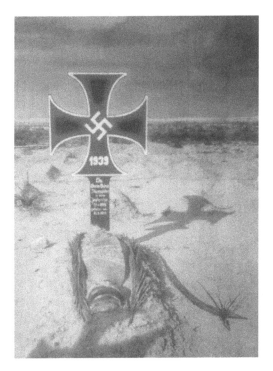

German burial (George Frame collection)

By the time we arrived in the vicinity of Tobruk the city was in our hands. The damage to the buildings told the sad story of what that place had endured over many years. There were many ships that had capsized in the harbour. The Germans had left sea mines that had to be destroyed so the port could be reopened.

Victims of bombing (George Frame collection)

Exploding the sea mines in the harbour. (George Frame collection)

At some point in all this action we got the news that the US army had invaded Morocco. This was celebrated with loud cheers and hugs between comrades in arms. I thought that with the US army in the battle, with their equipment and manpower, this desert war must soon be over. Rommel would now have to fight on two fronts and surely his Afrika Korps would be squeezed in the middle. However, when we heard that the French had fought the US Army in Morocco I thought what bastards they were. We were in this war as an ally of France and now they were fighting against us in support of the Germans who occupied their bloody country. I could not comprehend it. We had Free French on our side who had fought in the thick of it and other French were against us.

It was now mid November 1942 and Monty had won the battle of Al Alamein pushing Rommel back into Libya. The Germans and Italians were in full retreat with the bulk of the Eighth Army pursuing them. We found it hard to keep up.

Being back in Libya again we felt as if we knew our way around this desolate landscape. When we got to Gazala our orders were to travel south west to Msus. It seemed like a repeat performance and so, fuelled up and loaded with ammunition and supplies, we set off at a speedy pace.

The next day there was a sand storm which swept across our route. Rather than stop the CO wanted us to press ahead, which we did. I was sitting in the passenger seat of the truck and looked out to see a convoy travelling parallel to us. Then it just disappeared. I could not believe my eyes. Minutes later it reappeared. The vehicles in that convoy had passed behind a sand dune so it appeared as if they had disappeared. Then it struck me, as it did others, that they were Germans. What a fright to see the Germans so close. We immediately stopped, the CO yelling orders to the mobile anti-tank guns to engage and for us to uncouple the 6 pounders. The mobile guns swung around so their guns faced the column of enemy vehicles and fired. They missed each time they fired except the last shot hit an armoured car which went up in flames. Meanwhile we were scrambling to unhitch our gun. By the time we had done that the Germans were long gone. They did not want to engage in a fight and the CO elected not to pursue them.

Going to inspect what had been hit in any action was tricky in case the enemy lurked nearby. In this case the crew of this enemy vehicle were deceased. (George Frame collection)

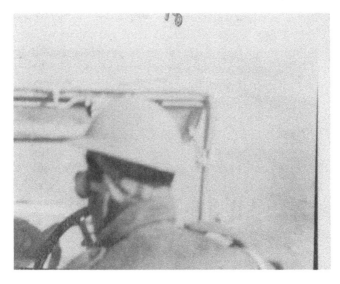

Driving in the dust and wind of the desert. (George Frame collection)

Along the way we discovered that wells had been soiled to make the water undrinkable. The Germans and Italians must have decided to do this to hinder our advance. Presumably they did not expect to be returning anytime soon.

Graves were scattered all over the place.

German, Italian and Allied dead buried together. (George Frame collection)

By the time we arrived at Benghazi the city had already been occupied by our chaps for several days. They must have raced across along the coast at one hell of a pace to get there. We were given time to rest up after we serviced the trucks and equipment. Getting a decent meal was a treat for us. Walter and I, plus a few other chaps, went to look around the city. The city was badly damaged from bombing. It must have been a lovely place with its architecture and wide streets. The port facilities had been wrecked by the retreating Germans.

Bengahzi from across the bay. (George Frame collection)

One of the few buildings in Benghazi that was intact. (George Frame collection)

The young locals must have been so frightened and confused as their towns were overrun by different nationalities. (George Frame collection)

When we got back we received an unexpected surprise. Guard duties of German prisoners! There were large numbers of German prisoners being assembled for transportation back to Egypt and we had to guard them in the open until the necessary transportation arrangements were arranged.

So I found myself standing with a rifle, along with a few other chaps, guarding these Germans. They looked dirty and bedraggled, reflective of the horrors they too must have been through. At one stage a big German soldier came close to me. His face was covered in dirt that looked like oil, and his uniform was torn in places. He had blond hair and bright blue eyes. I thought to myself this must be what the Arian race that Hitler wanted to rule the world looks like. In Southern Rhodesia I had never met any German people. He stared at me a long time then feigned an approach towards me. Like he was saying BOO. I instinctively stepped several paces back and raised my gun. He just smiled, turned his back on me and walked away. They could have easily stormed and overpowered us, but fortunately they did not. I wondered how they must feel, having fought us back and forth across this desert, being held as prisoner, not really knowing what fate lay ahead. Presumably they would be well treated as prisoners of war by the British and could look forward to staying alive as opposed to being buried in a sandy grave in this unrelenting place. I was not sure how our chaps who had surrendered to the Nazi's would be treated. The suspicion was that it would be bad. Anyway, I was relieved when my stint ended and thankfully I did not have to do any more guard duties.

German prisoners of war. (George Frame collection)

After leaving Benghazi we tracked west along the coastal road. We passed many of our tanks and transports along the way. Tanks running out of fuel was obviously a problem facing their commanders in keeping up with the chase across Libya. I recalled with vivid sadness being in this vicinity not that long ago digging graves for the fallen soldiers.

We re-joined the 7th south west of where the Germans had stopped near a place called Al Agheila. Preparations were being made to attack the German defensive positions. Once again we steeled ourselves for the battle. The problem was the same as before. Getting supplies of fuel and ammunition to the front lines got more problematic the further west we got. As was my habit I wrote letters to Lorraine and my parents and was unable to really sleep leading up to the next battle.

When the attack came it was preceded with the artillery barrage which we could hear to our north. Then the tanks advanced with us following up in the rear. Heavy fighting occurred ahead of us, lasting for hours, before the CO ordered us to prepare for engagement. We unhitched the guns and readied them. We discovered that we were actually very close to where the tanks had first engaged the enemy. As the day waned the battle still raged. Our advance had been foiled and as evening set in the enemy attacked us.

The rumbling of tanks coming towards us, growing ever more audible, kicked in the nerves and with thoughts of what may happen it was hard to supress the urge to run away. Firing into the darkness, we opened up along the entire row of anti-tank guns. Our best bet was to level the gun turrets and fire repeatedly hoping to hit something. A tank lit up.

Flares went up and I was able to see better through the field glasses. Jesus! There were many tanks ahead of us. I barked some instructions to the lads who were working like Trojans to keep the rate of fire up.

Fear hit me when, looking through the glasses, I saw flashes. The bloody tanks started firing at us. Another tank exploded, at the same time a barrage of incoming shells pelted us. It was truly frightening to see the flashes in the darkness, with shadowy silhouettes of burning tanks and hear the whistle of shells before they exploded.

Our tanks, which had been off to our right flank, engaged the enemy. After what seemed an agonisingly long time, the enemy withdrew into the darkness and with that an eerie silence descended upon us. My ears were ringing, I had sand in my eyes and I was shaking. The air smelt acrid, thick with smoke from the guns firing. An explosion from a burning tank startled me and one of our chaps dived under the truck. We all had our nerves shot to pieces. One of our guns had been hit and lads killed.

The next morning we had a brew up and some breakfast before we packed up to move on. The scene we came across told the story. Many destroyed enemy tanks but as we ventured further into the battle ground later in the morning we found several of our tanks that had been knocked out as well. Further along, we came across abandoned German vehicles and guns. They obviously must have retreated in a hurry.

German equipment abandoned. (George Frame collection)

Enemy stragglers were being rounded up only too eager to surrender. They had been through hell with the bombardments from the air force and artillery before the tanks had advanced. Remarkably I felt little anger towards them.

The enemy had been shattered and many only too willing to surrender

(George Frame collection)

It was not long before we suffered from lack of fuel which was being sent by land from Tobruk. Our supply lines were stretched to the limit and those of Rommel were shortening.

We heard that our forces had captured many German planes which I was told had been repainted and were now being used against the Germans. I reflected back to the day we shot down that Hurricane, killing the poor pilot, when we were told the Germans had captured our planes and were using them against us.

German aircraft were captured by advancing Allied forces. (George Frame collection)

If it came during the day you could see it approaching and try to prepare yourself. If it came at night that was a different story altogether.

The infamous dust storm!

Sand towering into the sky, swirling around, blanketing out everything. The noise was eerily nerve racking.

Once in the sand storm you could not see a thing. If someone was standing a few feet away they would become invisible. If driving in convoy, the trucks in front of you simply disappeared. You became totally disorientated. Sometimes breathing was difficult and you had to cover your mouth and nose with cloth. Wearing glasses was essential to save your eyes, as was covering up head to toe. The sand could shred your exposed skin as if you rubbed sandpaper on it.

The trucks and equipment would be caked in sand. It would get in everywhere and into everything. Often we had to dig our trucks out of the sand that had built up all around it once the storm had passed. The sand build up could be as high as the bonnet.

It was mid-afternoon that particular day and I was driving the supply truck with several lads in the back. Walter was in the cab with me. I was the third or fourth truck in a six truck convoy. Three of the trucks had the anti-tank guns in tow. We were told to keep a look out for any Germans or Italians who may have been overtaken by the advance and who would be trying to regroup with the other German forces in the west. We were aware that some of these stragglers had been captured quite easily as they appeared to have lost the backbone to fight. They were well and truly outnumbered and outgunned in any event. It was predicted many of the enemy would just surrender. But others had put up stiff resistance. Predictability was not something you took for granted.

We were driving along the winding track when the light took on an ominous colour. It was the sign that a sand storm was approaching. Fortunately it did not look like it was a monster but rather a more localised sand storm. Our Officer decided that we should continue as fast as possible to get to some place where he felt we could be better protected. I think he thought we could outrun the storm.

So we were belting along when the storm overtook us. I knew that was likely to happen. Because it was not a large full-blown sand storm we were not blacked out totally. But it soon became difficult to see the truck ahead of me. The sand was sweeping across the windshield in waves and the wind buffeted the truck. I felt relieved that I was in a supply truck as it had a closed in cab. The other trucks were open and the other lads in them would be getting belted.

Walter was giving me directions as to where the track was. I suspected he was more in the dark about what was ahead than I was. I lost sight of the track several times and then I lost sight of the truck ahead of me when, for many minutes, I was unable to see ahead at all. It was a sheet of sand.

Walter saw a vehicle off to his left and told me to turn left which I did. We followed that vehicle which was mildly visible for quite some time, over what was becoming rather rough terrain. I thought the fools in it had lost the track and were taking us all on a wild goose chase. Gradually the ferocity of the storm eased off, when all of a sudden, the wind died down and the sun shone through.

I was concentrating on the immediate ground ahead of the truck when Walter yelled out.

"Holy Mother of Mary! It's bloody Jerry!"

"Where?" I asked.

"The bloody truck ahead of us!"

And there they were. We were following two German transport trucks. Just at that time the canvas at the back of the truck in front of us began lifting up. The Germans in the back of that truck started rolling it up now that the storm had died down. They saw us. We saw them. I'm not sure who got the bigger fright, us or them. I veered right and we went bouncing off. I noticed that behind us was one of our trucks which I hoped would follow us. They did.

I was very keen to get us away from the Germans. The troops in the back of their trucks could easily start shooting at us while we were not in a position to shoot back. Walter was fumbling with his gun with the intention to shoot at them for whatever good that would have done.

Then a remarkable thing happened. The two Germans sitting at the back of the truck waved at us. Walter instinctively waved back before we went our separate ways. We managed to put some distance between us and the Germans before the remnants of the sand storm engulfed us once again. I was so relieved, but also flummoxed at what had just occurred.

After a while I stopped because there were sizeable rocks around and I did not want to puncture a tyre. When the storm once again died down we all got out. Walter relayed the story to those in the back of our truck, who had been oblivious to what had happened. The other truck pulled up. The chap driving it had been concentrating on following me so had not realised the situation until he saw the back of a German truck disappearing. He said he had got one hell of a fright as well. We came to the conclusion that the Germans were probably just wanting to get back to their own and avoid any more fighting.

We had no idea where we were. It was getting late in the afternoon and with the storm pretty much blown out we decided to find a place to make a brew and have a meal before moving off to another spot to sleep. We would look for the others in the light of a new day.

We did eventually find our group later the next day and relayed with eagerness our adventure which was far more exciting than what they had experienced. They had got totally disorientated, separated and lost, but had the good sense to stop, so when the storm subsided, they found each other before night set in.

A monster sand storm approaches. (George Frame collection)

At one point, a few days before Christmas, we met up with some chaps from the New Zealand division who were bringing re-supply to the Front. We raided the 'sweet jar' and went on our way with more food than we should have been given.

Christmas day came and went without incident or celebration. We spent that day driving further inland. The terrain was rocky with little vegetation. The column of tanks and trucks we joined spread as far as one could see. It was slow going as breakdowns were a regular occurrence that tended to stop the whole advance. The tracks had to be cleared of mines and booby traps that the retreating Germans were laying all over the place. The wells had also been compromised in this part of the country to render them unusable.

On the first of January 1943 we had stopped for a brew. It was so hot and dusty. I wandered off to relieve my bladder and came across a small patch of vegetation. Whilst it was really only a few bushes and grasses, it was the most beautiful sight I could recall seeing for a long time. I sat down in the middle of it for a while before I heard the chaps calling for me. My tea was only warm by then but that didn't matter to me. Later I wondered why that small patch of bushes and grasses had taken me aback and I thought perhaps I was going crazy. Having endured such a long time in the vastness of the desert and the horrible things being done to each other in this war, finding this piece of vegetation clinging to life reminded me of both the fragility of life and its resilience.

The patch of vegetation that I found so appealing – was I going nuts?

(George Frame collection)

We were on our way to Tripoli which had been occupied by the British forces. My understanding was that it was a large city with fine buildings and a big harbour that the Italians had built. The Boys in Blue had bombed it so I expected a lot of damage. Not knowing if the Germans and Italians would be defending it, and if so, whether that would involve us in street battles, I was both rather excited to get to see it yet apprehensive about what battle we would be engaged in. Being caught up in street to street fighting must be terrible.

As it turned out very little fighting took place and we saw no action. By the time we got to the city, at the end of January, the Eighth Army was in full occupation. I was surprised to see that there was not as much damage as would be expected, except near the harbour, which must have taken the main brunt of the air force raids. Damaged and half submerged ships were evident.

We were well and truly worn out from driving through the heat of the desert and all wanted time to restore ourselves. My overall condition and health was not that great. We were allocated a place to set up camp and we pitched our tents quickly, took time to wash and shave before setting off for a short visit to wherever we could find to get a drink and meal. The following day was the routine for servicing the guns and equipment and to restock on fuel and supplies.

Chaps marching through the liberated city. (George Frame collection)

The locals, mainly young children, harried us for money, or whatever we could offer, wherever we went. Most looked bedraggled, but perhaps not as bedraggled as we looked. I asked someone what they kept saying to us and was told that they were saying we were their best friends. I suspected they had been telling the Italians and Germans that same line a few days ago.

The bonus was that we received new clothing which was a relief given ours was pretty well worn out. I was able to get a size smaller as I had lost so much weight. Our food supplies improved in quantity and choice with the tinned food being supplied from America.

Chapter Nine

When sharp stabbing pains in my abdomen occurred I suspected it was from the different type of food upsetting my digestive system. I lay on my bunk bed in the tent feeling quite poorly, groaning to myself, hoping it would go away. The CO noticed this and sent me to the field hospital. I felt so unwell I didn't object. The doctor examined me remarking that I was skin and bones. When he pressed my lower right abdomen I yelled out in pain.

"Right Corporal", he said, "You need an operation to remove your appendix."

I was immediately sent to a hospital and upon arrival they rushed me through to be prepared for the operation. While lying on a stretcher in a large room full of soldiers I saw there were many lads there with severe wounds. I was not entirely sure if I wanted to be cut open, it didn't look that hygienic, so I asked the doctor if perhaps my operation could wait because I was in far less a pickle than some others there.

"Some of these poor chaps will be buried tomorrow. Do you want to join them?" he quipped.

When I was being wheeled to the operating theatre there was a short wait in a corridor. They brought a fellow on another trolley to go into the other operating theatre and I found myself staring at two bloodied bandaged stumps. He had no legs.

After the operation I found myself in a ward that was packed like sardines. The doctor eventually came to see me saying the operation was a success. He said I was lucky as the appendix was perforated and was about to burst. Any longer and I could have died. I felt far luckier than some of the chaps in the ward. Legs and arms amputated. Shrapnel wounds leaving horrible disfigurement. There were a few strapped down as they were 'bomb happy' with shot nerves.

All appeared as if it was going well with my recovery when on the second day after the operation I began passing blood in my urine. I thought the surgeon must have cut my bladder. When I showed the nurse she rushed off to get the doctor. The doctor certainly looked worried. He confirmed the bladder would not have been damaged during the operation. As my overall physical condition was poor the doctor told me I was to be transported to Tobruk for rest and recuperation and further examination as they were unsure of what was causing the bleeding. That sounded serious to me and I began to think how fate could play such a wicked twist. Perhaps I would not die from being shot, bayonetted or blown up, but rather from whatever was happening inside me?

Before I left, Walter came to give me my kit bag. It was an emotional parting as we hugged saying to each other unconvincingly that everything would be alright and we would soon be reunited. That did not happen for several years.

Walter was shot in the groin somewhere in Tunisia a few months later. He lost a testicle as a consequence, but not his life. He told me he deserved a DSO (Distinguished Service Order) medal because his dingis (his term for his sexual organs) were shot off (Dingis Shot Off).

The road trip back to Tobruk was uneventful. We travelled along the coast road. I slept during most of it. The food was fine. The bouncing around in the back of the truck caused some bleeding from the stitches. At Tobruk hospital they removed the stitches and a doctor examined me to find out why there was blood in my urine. That British doctor was unable to ascertain what the cause was so decided that I should be transported back to Alexandria by hospital ship. In the meantime I was to stay in recuperation.

Repairs being undertaken to telephone communications (George Frame Collection).

During this time I was able to go out to see the town. I got tired quite quickly so was unable to stay out long, but I did enjoy wandering the streets. There was a lot of damage and repairs were being done all around the place. The harbour in particular was badly damaged. It did seem that finally Rommel was defeated, even though the battle was still raging, now in Tunisia,

Tobruk harbour was terribly damaged. (George Frame collection)

View from hospital in Tobruk. (George Frame collection)

George at hospital. (George Frame collection)

When the hospital ship eventually arrived there was a mad rush to embark the ill and wounded. It was, however, a long process due to loading stretchers across the gang way. Once loaded, the ship wasted no time to make its way out of the harbour. I was allocated a cabin on an upper deck which I appreciated. As we left the harbour and headed eastwards we passed several burned out wrecks and a tanker that was still on fire. I guessed there was no point in trying to put it out.

Hospital ship. (George Frame collection)

The shipping was targeted by both sides. (George Frame collection)

I elected to stay on the open decks most of the time. We were told that when on deck to keep an eye out for submarines. I wondered what would happen if we saw one. Well, the next day I was staring out to sea and blow me down a submarine surfaced. I nearly had a heart attack. I thought we had had it, but it turned out to be British.

Tanker burning outside Tobruk. (George Frame Collection).

With little to do on board I found myself rather frustrated. Having been so much on edge and anxious in battle, although for me sporadic, I found it hard to settle. My thoughts migrated to my darling Lorraine and my family back in Rhodesia. They all seemed to have drifted so far away from me. A melancholy feeling stayed with me for a long time.

After embarking from the hospital ship at Alexandria I was taken to a hospital, where, after a brief examination, nothing happened before I was relocated several days later to another British hospital near the Suez Canal. This was an unlucky moment because had I been sent to a hospital with South African doctors they would have discovered that I was suffering from bilharzia. Bilharzia is a disease contracted from contact with rivers and dams in parts of Southern Africa where the body is infested with flukes that bore through the skin and into organs. They can lie dormant for years then suddenly start being active and multiply making a person very ill. Worst case, a person could die. With my yearning to be in the Rhodesian bush, I had often waded through rivers and streams. So this must have happened with me and now flukes were in my bladder. (I only discovered this when I got back to Durban months later).

Unfortunately the British doctors who did not know of this disease began treating me with the wrong medicine, penicillin, which temporarily stopped the bleeding after a few days, but it did not treat the disease.

Doctor, orderly and nurse staff. (George Frame collection)

Due to my poor physical state I was categorised with a down grade and because of my knowledge and experience in servicing trucks, was reassigned to a base job with the Engineers in Alexandria. The British chaps I found myself with in Alexandria were decent enough, but they complained about a lot of what to me were minor things given what I had seen others had been through. These chaps had it cushy and they did not see how lucky they were. Many of the chaps often skivvied out of as much work as they could, often arriving back at the workshop in the mornings hung over from the night before. It was here that I learned of the saying that 'The fellow had complained about not having any shoes until he met the chap without any feet!'

Time dragged on from day to day, week to week. I occasionally felt remorseful that I had this cushy job while others were still being blown to bits in Libya or Tunisia. I often wondered how the lads were doing hoping they would get through this war okay. News was not that forthcoming on what was occurring at the Front, but I did try to keep aware of events as best as I was able. However, after several weeks I was somewhat surprised with how I began to mentally distance myself from being back in that hell hole, in the expanse of nothingness, as opposed to being in Alexandria where life seemed to be going on as normal.

Alexandria; life progressed as if the war was a distant past event.

(George Frame collection)

Alexandria Bay.

(George Frame collection)

The news that Rommel was beaten and Tunisia was free of the German and Italian army was good to get. The war in North Africa was over! The celebrations in Alexandria that followed were joyous with a victory parade held. The section I was attached to did not participate.

The Scots were always up for participating in a parade.

(George Frame collection)

I did however attend the parade as part of the crowd and was swept up in the overall release of tension and joy that at least this conflict in Africa was now at an end and particularly that the British and Commonwealth Allies had won. The thoughts about all those who had lost their lives or who had been badly wounded and those scarred for life with memories of the horror of the fighting were swept away as the parade passed by over a few hours.

The Victory Parade in Alexandria to celebrate the defeat of the Axis in North Africa. (George Frame Collection).

When I learned that the Rhodesians could elect to join the South African Army and that the South Africans were getting home leave before going on to fight in Italy I rushed off to Cairo and joined up with the South Africans. It was quite a simple process which was surprising given my past experiences with the army and its red tape and processes. I had to return to the depot in Alexandria to sign off duty there and to say farewell to the chaps whom I had been with at the depot. What fortunate timing that was because within a couple of weeks I was on my way to Port Tewfik by train to await the troop ship that was going to take us back to Durban.

Oh joy to be able to get back and see my Lorraine! But as I had not heard from her for so long I was plagued with doubts. Was she still waiting for me or had she moved on?

Sharing a beer with lads at the depot in Alexandria. George lower right.

(George Frame collection)

At Port Tewfik we were billeted in a tent camp across the bay from the harbour. Soon after I arrived the South Africans also began arriving into the camp in waves. They had been through hell in so many battles. The stories that were relayed on what they saw and went through was really horrific. Many had gone right through all the fighting. How they remained sane was remarkable.

After a few days being pent up in the camp, many chaps became 'sun crazy'. We were desperate to get on the ship and go home. Every now and again someone would shout out that the ship was sighted and we would all rush around to look. Then, with immense disappointment, we would retreat back to the mundaneness of the camp life.

Then one morning, while I was dressing, I became semi-paralysed and could not pull up my trousers. Initially the chaps in my tent thought I was playing around until they realised something was actually wrong with me. They helped me get dressed and assisted me to the medical tent. The doctor, who was South African, examined me. He was most surprised that I had not complained of a sore throat. It had been sore for a long time but I had just accepted that. He said that I had rotten tonsils which were poisoning my system. They needed to be removed and he gave me two options. One was to return to Cairo to have the operation or he could give me some medicine that may help until I got back to Durban, where I would have the operation. There was no decision to be made. I was going back to South Africa.

I wrote letters to Lorraine and my parents and when I dropped them in the post sack, it dawned on me that the mail would probably go on the same ship that was taking us back!

When the ship eventually arrived it was certainly a terrific sight to behold. The Mauretania was its name. There was a rush to get us all to the port to board and as soon as the last person was aboard the ship set off. There was to be no lingering in the port which had several wrecks to remind us all about the war which was still real and no doubt the captain was aware that the fortunes in a war were unpredictable.

I was allocated a cabin with 7 others low down near the water line. It was hot as hell and we were not allowed to open the portholes. This was because if the ship was hit by a torpedo or a sea mine and listed to one side the open portholes would allow water in. I decided to repeat what I had done years before when being transported to this place and found a spot on deck. I spent most of my time there.

Our destroyer escort joined the ship the next day when we entered the Red Sea. It was a really attractive looking ship that hopefully would protect us all the way back to Durban. The risk of being torpedoed was ever present. The ship was carrying an awful lot of troops and she was travelling hell for leather. We were told that if any one fell overboard the ship would not stop. The ship must have been grand in its day but now, as a troop carrier over many years, it was looking very tired.

Troopships were protected – always vigilant

(George Frame collection)

183

I was unwell with a fever for several days, until the medicine began to work. The blood came back in my urine and with it I became concerned that I may not make it back to Durban. It worried me if I had made the right decision. I tended to sleep a lot of the time and missed some meals due to that. I didn't really mind as I was not that hungry anyway. The South African doctor on-board examined me and suggested I should have the tonsils out while on the ship. He said they were in a bad way. I declined because I didn't want to be laid up when we docked in Durban in a few days so he gave me more medicine. I mentioned the blood in the urine and after further poking and prodding he suggested I may have bilharzia and that I should have that looked at on shore as well.

The morning I awoke to see land emerging from the mists was absolutely glorious. The Bluff is a prominent hill feature at the entrance of Durban harbour and was the last thing I saw of Southern Africa many years before when we departed for Egypt. We were now safely back.

However once inside the Durban bay, and as the ship was being manoeuvred by the tugs to dock, the soldiers all pressed onto the one side of the ship. This caused the ship to list precariously towards the dock. The Captain announced that unless we dispersed evenly on deck he would have to order us all to our cabins and if we refused to do that he would take the ship out to sea. He did not have to repeat this warning.

It seemed like it took forever to dock the ship before we started the arduous disembarkation deck by deck, with paperwork galore. Then to face the gauntlet of MP's who were in numbers searching bags for things we were not allowed to have, like German guns, knives, and the like. I missed being selected, not that I had a German weapon. I did have an Italian flag, some badges, my camera, and the one I had found which I did not want to have confiscated.

Once past all the checks I looked for a public telephone and finding one, I phoned the Stuttafords store to speak to Lorraine. My heart was pounding in my ears as I waited to hear her voice. When I was put through to the department Lorraine worked in I was told by a woman that Lorraine had taken the day off. What disappointment!

Chapter Ten

What to expect? Would Lorraine still love me or had she moved on?

Swept along with a hoard of other soldiers to the gates at the end of the dock, my intent was to make my way as quickly as I could to Lorraine's parents' house. But when I got near the gate there she was standing behind the fence. She must have received a letter I had sent months before suggesting I was on my way back. What a lovely sight! My heart leapt out of my chest.

Once outside the gate I dropped my kit bag and hugged her. Tears ran down her face. I then knelt down and asked her to marry me. I had already asked her in a letter so long ago but I had not received a reply. Up to that moment I had not doubted I would marry Lorraine, but at that particular moment I held my breath. When she said yes I could not believe it and I had to ask again. It was the happiest moment in my life to that point. She did tell me later that she had received my letter asking her to marry me and she had replied yes. She said receiving that letter was the most wonderful surprise and it made her float on air. I never did get her letter.

What she saw in me as I stood in front of her I could not have guessed. I was a walking skeleton, sickly coloured and worn out. But she said yes!

We were given a week's leave, but I was supposed to report to the medical officer regarding my tonsils. I couldn't have cared less about my tonsils or the blood in my urine. All I wanted was to be with Lorraine. That glorious week passed in a flash and I felt that I was in a dream. Lorraine's father gave his permission for us to marry, while her mother tried to feed me as if I was a bullock being primed for slaughter. Lorraine's father was a gentle man whom I respected and liked even though I had not spent much time in his presence. He was a railway steam engine driver – a hard job.

It was a very sad day when I returned to the camp. The next day I went to see the doctor who took one look down my throat and ordered an immediate operation to remove the tonsils. I told Lorraine that I was off to the hospital in Durban and she came to visit me every day I was there. My throat hurt like hell after the operation and I was on medication for some time to clear up the infection. While in hospital the doctors tested my urine and confirmed bilharzia. They arranged for treatment to start the next week and I was transferred to a hospital annex.

Lorraine and George in Durban

(George Frame collection)

I did not know how painful the bilharzia treatment was going to be. Long needles injected into my abdomen every second day for two weeks. I soon got to a stage that I feared the nurse and doctor when they came to give me the injection. The only good thing was the regular visits from Lorraine and the news she had about her preparations for the wedding.

I got news that Wally had been shot but was alive and would be sent back home. Taffy was a prisoner of war with the Germans – poor chap.

When I told Lorraine that there was a possibility that I would be sent back with the South African Army to fight in Italy she wept. I did not want to go back. It was not an option to desert, so whatever fate lay ahead we agreed to set aside so as to focus on the wedding once I was released from hospital.

I was given leave for two weeks for the wedding and honeymoon.

George and Lorraine wedding in Durban, Republic of South Africa in September 1943

(George Frame collection)

The wedding was on a Saturday. The weather in Durban in September was lovely. I was as nervous as all hell and thankfully Lorraine's brother Desmond, who was my best man and also in the South African Army, managed to keep me calm and get me to the church on time.

Dressed in an Army uniform that was too big for me, a gaunt face and dark rings around my eyes, I must have looked a sorry sight. But my grin reflected how utterly happy I was that day. And when I turned to see Lorraine walking down the aisle holding on to her father's arm, dressed in her lovely white laced wedding dress, my knees literally gave way. Desmond had to steady me. The rest was a blur. When I look at the pictures of the wedding I can see how happy an occasion it was.

We did not have much money, I was broke after buying a modest wedding ring. Lorraine's parents were not wealthy, having raised nine children, but we had a nice reception with a small gathering.

We set off by train for Bulawayo, Southern Rhodesia, so I could introduce my bride to my family. It was just wonderful to be with the women I truly loved and terrific to be able to look out the train window and see trees, grass and fields of crops. Even travelling through Botswana and western Rhodesia, where the countryside was dry and brown, was a joy compared to that dreadful desert.

At Bulawayo train station, my mother, father and two brothers, Harold and Douglas, were there to meet us. How wonderful it was to see them all again and to be able to introduce them to my wife. We stayed with my parents at the family house on the outskirts of Bulawayo, a house my mother had built with black Rhodesian labourers and blood, sweat and tears over many years. The time flew past and we were soon back on the train station platform saying goodbye. It was a sad occasion indeed because the uncertainty of the war, and where I was going to be sent, hung over us all.

Every moment was so precious with Lorraine. I hoped the train trip back to Durban would take forever. But our time together came to an abrupt end when, the day after we got back to Durban, I had to report for duty at Hay Paddock, Pietermaritzburg, some miles north of Durban. The parting was dreadful because the South African Army redeployment back to the war in Europe had already commenced and I was uncertain as to when I would be sent away.

When I arrived at the new army camp I was immediately rostered for a medical. I failed. They categorised me Grade C – fit only for base duties. Trying not to look ecstatically happy was jolly hard, but it was a very happy day for me indeed. Once out of ear shot I let off big cry of joy. That afternoon I managed to evade the guards and left the camp making my way back to Durban to see Lorraine. She burst into tears when I told her the news. We both hugged with the joy of it. There was a possible hitch though. Grade C could be posted to a war zone and that meant I still may end up in Italy.

I had to get back before the roll call so our meeting was brief. My plan was to go back to the camp by bus but when I approached the bus stop I stopped in disbelief. There was the Medical Officer waiting for the bus! I then had to wait an hour for the next bus which made it very tight to get back. I scooted around to the other side of the camp and clambered over the wire fence without getting hooked on the barbed wire. I just made it. Others who had gone AWOL and who were caught were immediately sent to Durban to be transported to Egypt. I thought to myself afterwards how stupid I was to risk that for a few hours with Lorraine and how close I came to having been caught.

It was an anxious time for me because there was still the chance I was going to be sent back to the war. Being in a base in a war zone had its risks, even if they were less than those poor souls at the Front. Bases could be bombed and if the enemy got the upper hand, they could even be overrun.

I waited anxiously to receive my papers that would seal my fate. When I was handed the brown envelope my hands shook. I pealed back the envelope and took out the letter. I found it hard to read because I was shaking so much. The letter said that I was to be discharged from the South African Army in favour of transferring to the Southern Rhodesia Regiment.

What did that mean? I asked the Warrant Officer if he knew and he said "You are going back to Southern Rhodesia!"

I was so overjoyed. I managed to get a day pass to meet Lorraine and explain what was happening. We arranged to meet in a lovely park in Pietermaritzburg. Lorraine brought a picnic basket. There were several people at the park that prevented us having much of a cuddle. We talked about our plans now that the future had been set for us. We agreed that I would arrange for Lorraine to travel up to Southern Rhodesia once I was redeployed there.

The next day I boarded a train for Pretoria where I had to go through a process to be discharged from the South African Army. This process, with all the paperwork and waiting around, took a very long while. I nearly missed the train that was to take me to Salisbury, via Bulawayo, where I had to present myself to the Rhodesia Regiment HQ. I telegraphed my mother to tell her I was coming home and managed a quick hello with her on the station platform in Bulawayo before the train left for Salisbury. She was delighted as was I that I was not being sent back to the war. I arranged for Lorraine to stay with my parents when she came to Southern Rhodesia and until I knew exactly what duties and location I would find myself.

Arriving in Salisbury I was taken to the army barracks to be enrolled into the Rhodesia Regiment. The question I had asked myself was, seeing that I was a volunteer rather than a conscript into the army, why could I not just be discharged. When I mentioned this I was told very emphatically that I had joined up and had to serve it out no matter how long it took regardless that there was no conscription in Rhodesia. I had another medical that also gave me a base duty classification. I was kitted out, billeted in the army barracks in Salisbury and assigned to Army Ordinance Stores in a clerical role. After two months I was given two week's leave to travel by train to Durban to fetch Lorraine to take her to Bulawayo.

It was a sad day for her to leave her parents to travel far north to a strange land and to stay with people she had only met for a few days. She had never lived anywhere other than at her parents' home. There were lots of tears when she said goodbye to her mother and father and a few of her sisters on the train platform in Durban. There were more tears all the way to Bulawayo as well.

I briefly settled Lorraine in at my parents' home before returning to Salisbury where I began a search for rented rooms so we could set up home together. I was unsure how Lorraine and my mother would get on and I did not want to chance leaving her there with mother too long. I managed to buy a green Morris 8 two door car, with help again from my father, and so each weekend I raced off to Bulawayo to be with Lorraine. Thankfully it appeared to be okay on the domestic front in Bulawayo.

Reasonably priced accommodation was not easy to find but I did manage to find something suitable and when I brought Lorraine to Salisbury, we settled into our married life together. Money was very tight but fortunately Lorraine got a job at the main Department store, Barbour's, earning twice what I was paid. We saved like mad because we wanted to buy our own house one day. When the municipality began selling land stands with newly built 2 bedroom houses for ex-servicemen with a twenty five year fixed interest repayment scheme there was a lot of interest. There were limited stands available and many applications being made. We applied and with the assistance of Mr Barbour himself, who was a counsellor, we were awarded one in Eastlea.

Life together was wonderfully good. Lorraine settled into her job and was well thought of by management. I had a job that was clerical. It was not that difficult in maintaining ordinance store records. My health recovered and I started to look and feel well.

Lorraine got used to my nightmares which, over time, became less frequent.

Married life. George and Lorraine

(George Frame collection)

George's Medals and Insignia

Medals: (from left): Southern Rhodesia George VI. D. G. B
OMN-REX-ET-INDIA-IMP,

South African Africa Service Medal, British George VI. D. G. B
OMN-REX-ET-INDIA-IMP.

Medals: (from left): The 1939-1945 Star, The Africa Star.

Uniform Insignia

Rhodesia Regiment Inginia

George's Eighth Army 'Dog Tags'

Chapter Eleven

George found a camera when looking through abandoned German vehicles.

When he managed to get the film developed he found the following:

Rommel

The following pictures were given to George by lads he met up with in the desert:

Italian's surrendering after the battle of Beda Fomm

German's surrendering

Chapter Twelve

It was the summer of 1976 when George took Lorraine and me, his son John, to Europe for a holiday.

We were in Frankfurt which was experiencing an unseasonal heat wave. The Rhine was at its lowest level in a decade and we had been informed that the boat that we were going to board in a few days to travel to Amsterdam may be unable to return back.

We spent a morning at the Frankfurt botanical gardens and were delighted at how magnificent and extensive they were. The rows of garden beds flourishing with terrific flowering plants was truly stimulating. Some displays were awe-inspiring. It was a thoroughly enjoyable morning that had spilt over into early afternoon.

After leaving the gardens we went in search of somewhere to get a meal and something cold to drink. It had been hard to get any cold drinks in the past few days which made us wonder if the Germans had any refrigeration anywhere. Perhaps it was just our bad luck?

We stumbled across a place that looked nice enough to get a meal. There were plenty of people in the restaurant and the scene looked festive. We were shown to a table outside the main restaurant which we were grateful for as it was hot and sticky inside. At least outside there was a slight breeze and we were under an awning.

My father was desperate for a drink so ordered a beer for himself and me. My mother opted for a Coke. Two large pale looking beers arrived and the Coke – all warm, not cold. Disappointment swept over us before, out of desperation and being so thirsty, we drank and reordered this time asking for ice to be put into the drinks. We got the drinks without ice.

The beer didn't seem to have much punch in it so my father had a few. After going to the gent's toilet he tripped over a chair and stumbled into the table of people sitting next to us. They had been having a very merry time. Apologising profusely my father got into a conversation with a man about his own age. He spoke English reasonably well so the communication between them was okay. We could not speak any German at all.

The two men seemed to be getting on famously, chatting away and gesticulating, as if shooting at something. My mother asked me if George may be getting himself into a pickle because the Germans were the enemy and lost the war. She hoped George was not reminding them of that.

Then suddenly this man stood up which made my mother and me flinch, thinking there was a problem to then be bemused and rather taken aback when they both hugged, slapping each other on the back. After that show of emotion, George finally introduced us to the man he was talking with. It turned out that he had been a 109 pilot during the war and had been in the desert at the same time George was there. George had recounted how the 109's had shot at them and this man had recounted how he had shot at the English. He had survived the desert war and was posted to Germany to shoot down American Flying Fortresses. He had been shot down over the Ruhr and, while being able to bail out, was badly injured so was unable to fly again.

That night I asked dad what all that was about. How could he embrace someone who had killed men who were on his side of the war?

"Time heals almost everything," he told me.

He said he felt better for hugging the man. The next day he didn't feel better. He had one almighty hangover.

Map of North Africa

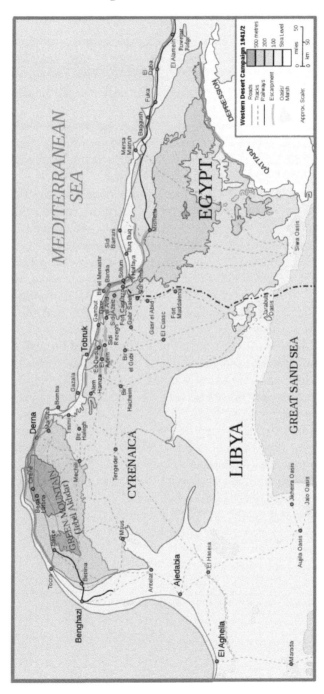

Epilogue

George was 93 in 2009. He lived in a house within a retirement village, still independent and was thoroughly happy with his circumstance. Lorraine had passed in 2004 which he said was like someone had ripped his heart out of his chest. He missed her terribly but had accepted that life goes on.

He had never chosen to talk much about the Second World War and only had shared snippets of information sparingly. But in recent times he had begun to talk about aspects of the war in which he had participated in North Africa as a Desert Rat in the Eighth Army.

I took notes so as to try and capture this history of my father and to relay this one day to his grandchildren. It is so easy to loose history and I sincerely believe that we are fortunate to live as we do today because of the selfless sacrifices of those who fought tyranny and evil.

George held no hatred for the Germans or Italians. He actually admired the Germans for their manufacturing quality and resilience to rebuild their society after it was shattered and destroyed by the Allies during that war.

George did however question the futility of war and mused at how things change so quickly.

He reminded me of when, in 1976, we had passed through Checkpoint Charlie into East Berlin and saw the wall, tank traps and armed troops, that the USSR which had been an ally in the Second World War was now the enemy. West Germany who had been the enemy was now the ally. Japan was the close ally of the USA, yet China and Russia were no longer friendly towards the USA or UK. He explained to me that the whole business of war seemed to be a futile exercise in human insecurity, greed and ego. He drew the comparison to what we in Rhodesia at that time were experiencing with a civil war ranging and questioned after it's all done, will those who were once enemies be friends?

George believed that he had lived a wonderful life.

He passed away peacefully at the age of 94 in 2010 after a short heart related illness.

George Frame

(27/03/1916 - 05/07/2010)

George was born on 27th September 1916 in Gwelo, Southern Rhodesia. He was the second of three boys.

His father, Francis, was a mining engineer who had left the hardship of mining in the United Kingdom for the new colony of what was to be called Southern Rhodesia. Founded by a special charter granted by Queen Victoria to Cecil Rhodes, the British South Africa Company sought mineral concessions north of the Limpopo River from the Matabele King, Lobengula. Soon thereafter in 1893-4, a war between the Company's soldiers and Lobengula's Matabele warriors saw the Company take administrative control of the land between the Limpopo and Zambezi. That land became known as Southern Rhodesia.

With new mineral discoveries being found, mines were established and George's father was attracted to those opportunities.

Life in Southern Rhodesia in 1916 was hard. A new civilisation was being carved out of the raw bush. There was a general lack of many things, especially any luxuries. Life on the mines was particularly basic and tough.

George's mother resented being dragged from England to the wilderness of Southern Africa. She longed to return to Lancashire where she kept a house, waiting for their return, for many decades, something that never eventuated. She did however refuse to move around from mine site to mine site and so put her roots down in Bulawayo, where she built a family home.

The three boys lived with their mother in Bulawayo while their father moved about working on mine sites.

George was the middle son and was the most difficult for his mother to manage. He was always disappearing to the bush looking for birds, reptiles and the like. In his youth the bush was dangerous. Wildlife abounded and the herds of antelope would always attract the big cats; Lion, Leopard and Cheetah. The buffalo were also dangerous, as were Hippo and Crocodiles in the lakes and rivers. Most snakes were venomous. So George's mother lived on tenterhooks when he sneaked off.

The boys initially went to Milton Boys School in Bulawayo as day scholars. George was a poor student, getting the cane frequently. His interest in scholarly pursuits was overshadowed by his interest in the outdoors.

His mother, in the hope to get back to England and to instil some education into her boys, sent them to the Lancashire Royal Grammar

School. So at 7 years of age George went by train to Cape Town to catch a Union Castle ship to Southampton in England and then a train to Lancashire to attend boarding school.

George emulated his poor scholarly performance at the Lancashire Royal Grammar School and the occasional incidents occasioning corporal punishment by way of a cane continued. This was a very difficult period for George. His aunt in Lancashire who looked after the boys at the school breaks wrote to his mother saying she refused to look after George, who she said was a scallywag and a rascal.

George was repatriated back to Southern Rhodesia after a few years and went back to Milton where he managed to fit in, completing his high school without any distinction or qualification as a secondary interest to his outdoor bush activities. He did however enjoy rugby which was played on largely gravel playing fields and as a consequence he carried perpetual scars on his knees and elbows.

After leaving school, George secured several labouring roles on a mine site in Northern Rhodesia. He took work on a mine in Northern Rhodesia when his father moved there to work on the mines. His mother, bitterly unhappy at being taken to Northern Rhodesia, refused to stay so went back to Bulawayo. Later when George contracted sickness she travelled to fetch him back home.

After he recovered from his illness he took a labouring job at a large meat processing abattoir.

As a young adult, George enjoyed dancing and would eagerly go to local dances that were held. He was a social character and well liked.

When Britain declared war on Germany on 3rd September 1939, Southern Rhodesia issued its own declaration of war almost immediately, before any of the dominions did. It was not long after that George started talking about volunteering to enlist, but his mother was dead against it. She had vivid memories of the carnage in the First World War and did not want her sons slaughtered. However, the time came when George volunteered and joined the Rhodesia Regiment. He was enthusiastic to enlist because he was at a loss in what his career or life path was.

The period from his enlistment to the end of the war is the subject of this story.

After the war George settled into a blissful married life with Lorraine in their two bedroom house in Eastlea, Salisbury, Southern Rhodesia. After being discharged from the Rhodesia Regiment at the end of the war, George found work in a clerical capacity as a depot manager for Texaco. Lorraine continued to work at Barbours Department Store earning more than George – a job she kept until her first child arrived. Thereafter Lorraine remained a stay at home mother.

A package of joy arrived in 1946, when Diann was born. John arrived eight years later and with that new family addition George built an extension to the house to add a 3rd bedroom and a garage.

With Lorraine stopping work, George needed to find better employment and to that end, he met up with three other men to form a Company that was called Puzey & Diss Motors which was successful in securing the British Motor Corporation franchise for Southern and Northern Rhodesia. George's role was to manage the spares department, something his time in the army ordinance had taught him to handle. He remained with that company until 1983 when he retired at the age of 67, before emigrating to join John in Australia. In 1976 George sold his shares in that Company and with the proceeds he was able to finally feel financially comfortable. The payout allowed George to build his 'dream house' in Newlands, Salisbury and to earn dividends from the investment of the balance.

Prior to this pay out, the money was tight, but regardless, Lorraine managed the home budget with expert diligence. The family lived a modest life without extravagance. George believed in family holidays and each year he would take the family by car, taking two days, to Durban for a three week holiday, essentially so that Lorraine could visit with her large family.

He maintained his passion for birds, keeping aviaries of various species for many years.

In the early 1960's, when the United Kingdom began disengaging from its Empire, the political situation in Central Southern Africa became filled with controversy and tension. George joined the Police Reserve and was called to attend when riots broke out in the Black Rhodesian townships. The chaos and the one party state Governments that were being formed with newly independent states to the north of Southern Rhodesia crystallised his political views at this time. He believed in the view that a responsible government took precedence over a blanket voting franchise.

The Southern Rhodesian situation in the British Empire was not straight forward. Having been granted its own constitution for self-Government in 1924, the Government of the United Kingdom reneged on undertakings previously given to the Southern Rhodesian Government regarding its independence. This led to a Unilateral Declaration of Independence by the Government of Rhodesia in November 1965, the imposition of United Nations sanctions against it and the start of a bitter 13 year civil war that culminated in the formation of Zimbabwe in early 1980.

George was too old to be subjected to the civilian call up during the civil war, but he took an active interest in the political affairs within the ruling political party, The Rhodesian Front.

His family managed not to fall victim to the revenges of that war. His daughter, Diann, lived with her family on a farm and fortunately were not attacked. His son-in-law, Russell, served in the Police Anti-Terrorist Unit seeing action on many occasions. His son, John, served in the Rhodesian Air Force for two years.

After the Marxist Government was installed with the formation of Zimbabwe, his daughter and family left their farm for South Africa. A year later his son and his wife immigrated to Australia. Torn between the two children living in different countries thousands of kilometres apart, George and Lorraine joined John and his wife, Janet, in Australia in 1983. He immediately adopted that country as his own. Leaving Zimbabwe with limited assets due to the restrictions imposed by the country's Government, he was nonetheless able to buy a modest house with a bank loan. Relying on a diminishing pension payment from Zimbabwe and by living modestly, he was able to pay off the loan.

His daughter Diann and her husband, Russell, eventually immigrated to Australia to reunite the family.

George had a very positive influence on his grandchildren as he had on his children by teaching them base human values and constantly affirming their worth.

Lorraine passed in 2004, an event that he described as "having my heart ripped out from my chest". He however managed to live independently with a positive attitude towards life until in 2010 his heart gave out.

His ashes are laid to rest next to those of Lorraine at the base of a Tuart Tree at Pinnaroo Cemetery, Perth, Western Australia.

GEORGE RICHARD FRAME

Born in Rhodesia – 27 3 1916

Beloved Husband of Lorraine

And father of Diann and John

A Wonderful Life Lived Honestly

A true Friend Sadly Missed

Reunited with Lorraine – 5 7 2010

A Love Story With No Ending

I will Love You Forever Lorraine

His mantra in the latter part of his life was **"It's a wonderful Life!"**

About the Author

John was born in Salisbury, Rhodesia. (Harare, Zimbabwe).

Having achieved a Bachelor of Commerce at Rhodes University in the Republic of South Africa majoring in Accounting, Business Administration and Commercial Law, John was invited to undertake an Honours Degree in Accounting.

He returned to Rhodesia and after serving several years with the Rhodesian Air Force during the Rhodesian civil war, he trained as a Chartered Accountant with Price Waterhouse in Zimbabwe and then in Australia.

John has been in several senior executive roles in companies operating in many different industries.

John is an author of *Retribution*, published in 2014, a thrilling historical fiction novel set in war torn Rhodesia, the *Paradigm of Success*, which is guide to personal effectiveness and in 2018 *The Rhodesian Civil War (1966-1979)* history book.

John has a strong focus on his family and lives in Australia.

Bibliography

Chris Frame – Georgic www.chriscunard.com

Desert War: The North African Campaign 1940-1943 by Alan Moorehead (Penguin Books -2001)

George Frame Second World War Diaries and Photographs

German Tanks of World War II: 1939-1945 by David Porter (Amber Books – 2019)

Images of War. British Tanks in Second World War by Pat Ware (Pen and Sword Books – 2011)

John Frame diary notes

Rommel in North Africa: Quest for the Nile by David Mitchelhill-Green (Pen and Sword Books - 2017)

A 'Desert Rat' Story

Lightning Source UK Ltd.
Milton Keynes UK
UKHW020226150122
397153UK00006B/171